ROGER HUNT studied stage management at drama school and has worked in film, television and photography. A major turning point in his life was attending a weekend homeowners' course run by the SPAB. Loving history and having been intrigued by building techniques and materials since childhood, he then started writing about old buildings and their construction. He now contributes to magazines on old and new buildings, history and, more recently, sustainability issues. He is the author of *Rural Britain: Then & Now*, *Villages of England* and *Hidden Depths: an archaeological exploration of Surrey's past*.

MARIANNE SUHR, MRICS, SPAB Lethaby Scholar, is a Chartered Building Surveyor specialising in the repair of historic buildings. After completing a scholarship with the SPAB she worked for seven years in architectural practice, then concentrated on hands-on repair projects including three very different old houses. She was a co-presenter of three series of BBC2's *Restoration* and has also fronted the Discovery TV series *Project Restoration*. She works part-time for the SPAB, running workshops around the country, teaching builders, homeowners and architects how to repair old buildings properly.

THE SOCIETY FOR THE PROTECTION OF ANCIENT BUILDINGS was founded by William Morris in 1877 to counteract the highly destructive 'restoration' of medieval buildings being practised by many Victorian architects. Today it is the largest, oldest and most technically expert national pressure group fighting to save old buildings from decay, demolition and damage. Members include many leading conservation practitioners, homeowners living in houses spanning all historical periods and those who simply care about old buildings.

OLD HOUSE HANDBOOK

A PRACTICAL GUIDE TO CARE AND REPAIR

Roger Hunt & Marianne Suhr

In association with
THE SOCIETY FOR THE PROTECTION OF ANCIENT BUILDINGS

FRANCES
LINCOLN

Dedication

For Elizabeth and Molly, my late aunt, for their encouragement ROGER HUNT
For Bob and Yvonne, to whom I owe all my achievements MARIANNE SUHR

Brimming with creative inspiration, how-to projects and useful
information to enrich your everyday life, Quarto Knows is a
favourite destination for those pursing their interests and passions.
Visit our site and dig deeper with our books into your area of interest:
Quarto Creates, Quarto Cooks, Quarto Homes, Quarto Lives,
Quarto Drives, Quarto Explores, Quarto Gifts, or Quarto Kids.

Old House Handbook:
A Practical Guide to Care and Repair

© 2017 Quarto Publishing plc

Foreword © 2008 Philip Venning
Text © 2008 Roger Hunt & Marianne Suhr
Edited and designed by Jane Havell Associates

First Published in 2008 by Frances Lincoln,
an imprint of The Quarto Group.
The Old Brewery, 6 Blundell Street,
London N7 9BH, United Kingdom.
T (0)20 7700 6700 F (0)20 7700 8066
www.QuartoKnows.com

A catalogue record for this book is available from
the British Library.

ISBN 978 0 7112 2772 9

Printed and bound in China

Front cover and background of back cover
© Nerijus Juras/Shutterstock

Contents

THE SOCIETY FOR THE PROTECTION OF ANCIENT BUILDINGS

The Society for the Protection of Ancient Buildings was founded by William Morris in 1877 to counteract the highly destructive 'restoration' of medieval buildings being practised by many Victorian architects. Today it is the largest, oldest and most technically expert national pressure group fighting to save old buildings from decay, demolition and damage.

Members include many of the leading conservation practitioners as well as home owners, living in houses spanning all historical periods, and those who simply care about old buildings. Thousands of buildings survive which would have been lost, mutilated or badly repaired without the SPAB's intervention. Indeed, many of the most famous structures in Britain are cared for by some of the several thousand people who have received the Society's training.

The SPAB is not a learned body, nor is it a champion of any one style or period. Instead, it is a charity representing the practical and positive side of conservation, not only campaigning but educating and offering advice. Courses are run for building professionals and home-owners and information is available in the form of publications and a telephone helpline manned by experts.

A firm set of principles backed by practical knowledge, accumulated over many decades, is at the heart of the Society's approach to repair. Misguided work can be extremely destructive and the skill lies in making repairs with the minimum loss of fabric and so of beauty and authenticity – old buildings are not best preserved by 'restoring' them to make them new and perfect.

Remember, maintenance is the most practical and economic form of preservation. Buildings cannot be made to last for ever but, by the abstemious approach advocated by the SPAB, they will survive as long as possible and suffer the least alteration.

More information about the Society's work and the help it can offer is available at www.spab.org.uk.

William Morris (1834–96), founder of the Society for the Protection of Ancient Buildings.

Foreword

'If only we'd known before we started . . .' is something we hear all too often at The Society for the Protection of Ancient Buildings. So a warm welcome for this book, which draws on the practical experience of the SPAB over the last 130 years. It shows clearly how old houses can be repaired and adapted for the world of today, and indeed tomorrow, without sacrificing those subtle, fragile qualities of age and beauty that characterise our rich variety of historic buildings. The basic message is the same, whether your building is large or small, ancient or more recent. The book's aim is simple: to help homeowners hand down their houses 'instructive and venerable to those that come after us', to quote the Society's Manifesto written by William Morris in 1877.

The country still has thousands of houses that are 400 years old and more. The best way to ensure that the buildings we value today will still be enjoyed in another 400 years is to recognise the importance of tried and tested materials and craftsmanship; and to adopt the very best design in both their repair and adaptation. Above all, the book shows in practical terms why the careful and conservative repair of historic fabric, even if worn and a bit battered, is more sustainable than its needless replacement. Of course, this book can give only general guidance and homeowners will need to do their own research. But with it as a starting point you should avoid some of the most common mistakes, which are often costly and permanently damaging to the building itself. Future generations will thank you.

PHILIP VENNING
Secretary, SPAB

Please note that the information given here is based on the best current practice. But every building is different, and so specific recommendations or suggestions may not necessarily be relevant in every instance. They should not be applied automatically. If you are in any doubt, do seek suitably experienced professional advice. This also relates to the photographs and illustrations which indicate an approach, but which should not be treated as a guarantee of the correct method in every set of circumstances.

Research is a vital part of any work to an old building. The SPAB website, bookshop and advice line are geared towards helping homeowners, craftspeople and professional advisers and can provide the latest information. For this reason, lists of organisations, suppliers and publications that might quickly date have not been included here.

Listed building consent

Given the vast number of different areas of work covered in this book, it would be difficult, if not repetitive, to draw attention to all the circumstances in which consent may be required to make changes. This omission does not mean that the matter should be disregarded. Quite the contrary; the UK has strict laws which protect historic buildings, areas, sites and landscapes and it is in your interest to adhere to these.

Before beginning any work of repair, alteration or development to your house, any structures within its grounds or the site on which it stands, it is essential to check with your local planning authority whether any consent will be needed. In the case of all listed buildings, do remember that the interior as well as the exterior is protected, and that the listing may extend to ancillary structures within the main building's *curtilage* (the land attached to it). When consent is granted, work must follow the approved drawings exactly, as well as any conditions that have been imposed.

Preface

Whether you want simply to maintain an old building or are taking on a wreck in need of major work, there is no shortage of information available; the problem is that much of the advice is outdated, overly invasive or simply lacks detail. The aim of this book is to offer an alternative, highly practical approach with simple 'nuts and bolts' guidance based on experience. Importantly, we are keen to help you get it right first time round, rather than have to live with the consequences of expensive and potentially irreversible 'mistakes'.

Everyone who takes on an old building has different degrees of interest or skills and not all jobs are advisable for the untrained, even for the seemingly most dextrous. This is why we have packed some chapters with useful practical advice where readers can 'get their hands dirty' while, in other areas, we explain the points to think about when employing tradespeople and professionals.

In line with the SPAB's thinking, we emphasise the importance of repair and maintenance rather than restoration or replacement. We also point to ways in which the building may be enjoyed as a twenty-first century home, yet one that retains the character and idiosyncrasies associated with its past. With this in mind we hope you will find the following pages an indispensable and thought-provoking read, whether the house you have chosen is an early timber-framed cottage or an Edwardian terrace. And, rest assured, we know the pain, hard work and sleepless nights that you may have along the way – we have been there, done it and lived to tell the tale!

ROGER HUNT
MARIANNE SUHR

Look before you leap

Opposite: Derelict old houses are becoming rarer; they can be a dream project but before committing yourself think very carefully about the amount of time and thought needed to achieve a successful outcome both for you and for the building.

Right: Old houses have huge appeal. When undertaking any work it is important to consider what it is that makes the building special; take care not to strip away its 'character'.

Below: If carefully maintained and gently repaired, old buildings simply become more beautiful with time.

Old buildings are a precious and finite resource. Whether early stone structures, thatched cottages, manor houses, Georgian town houses or Victorian terraces, they have a character and quality quite different from anything built today; as a consequence, great care must be taken with repairs and alterations.

Buying any house, particularly an old one, tends to be an emotional rollercoaster, so try to prevent your heart ruling your head. Can you cope with uneven plaster-work, sloping floors and potentially draughty doors and windows? If you prefer perfect surfaces, level lines and double glazing, an old building (and this book) may not be for you.

Old buildings are valuable aesthetically, socially and historically and many occupiers see themselves as guardians rather than owners. When damage occurs, it is frequently more through ignorance than deliberate intent; using the right materials and techniques will save you trouble and even money in the long run.

It is worth remembering that a house that has been carefully repaired in sympathy with its age and style is always more likely to appeal to future purchasers than one that has been modernised at the expense of its history. This does not mean that old buildings have to be preserved in aspic: they simply need to be respected, and any improvements that are made need to be sympathetic to the building's needs. The golden rule is to do as little as possible and no more than is necessary.

ESSENTIAL CHARACTER

One of the reasons we like old buildings is because they have 'character', a subtle, intangible quality that has to do with texture, irregularity and the patina of age – history built up over many years.

Most buildings earlier than the first half of the nineteenth century followed the logic of their location, the dictates of materials and the skills of the period. Traditional builders were incredibly resourceful: with just a horse and cart at their disposal, everything needed to build a house was usually sourced within a five-mile radius, if not in the ground beneath their feet. The materials were natural, obtained from woodland, field and quarry. This use of local materials, combined with regional traditions and techniques, contributed to the development of a rich diversity of vernacular styles.

With the coming of canals and later railways, transportation of goods from one place to another became common and regional variations less marked. Even so, Victorian and Edwardian terraces, and many other houses of these times, display the attributes of character common to all old buildings.

WHAT TO LOOK FOR

Location is frequently cited as top of the list when buying a house. With old buildings there are many other important questions you should consider. Most fundamental is whether the building offers the right space and layout.

Countless converted churches, schools and barns show how awkwardly conventional domestic subdivisions sit within the generous open spaces of single-volume buildings. Similarly, original room divisions are not to be discarded lightly. Major rearrangements of the plan or inappropriate quick fixes are rarely successful. Attempts to make a simple house grand not only destroy the history and integrity of the building but will invariably diminish the attributes which attracted you to it in the first place.

Though rare these days, the most exciting old buildings are those where little has been done in the way of 'modernisation'. Their original plasters, finishes, roofs, floors, windows, doors and idiosyncrasies add character and are far easier to repair than those that have been inappropriately restored. Remember that cement-rich renders, layers of plasterboard and recent additions not

Is an old house right for you?

Before you get seduced by the idea of living in an old house ask yourself:

> Does an old house really suit you, your family and your way of life?
> Does the space work without making too many, if any, changes to the historic layout?
> Are you prepared for the draughts, the spiders and that niggling damp spot that may never go away?
> Can you cope with low doors and beams that you bang your head on?
> Can you get your favourite wardrobe up the stairs?
> Can you afford to carry out the work that will almost certainly cost more than you planned and maybe more than the house is worth?
> Are you ready for the maintenance hassles that come with old buildings?

Above: The vernacular tradition is epitomised in this little croft in the Orkney Isles, a building entirely the product of its location – it is even orientated to cope with the forces of nature.

Right: The idea of buying an old house is seductive but there are many practical considerations to take into account before making the commitment.

Do your homework before you buy

Before buying an old house it is essential to gather all the facts:

> Find out why the present owners are selling. They may know something that you don't!

> Get a full survey carried out by people who specialise in the type of building you are considering. Don't be afraid to ask for proof of their experience.

> The possibility of liability means that surveyors point out rather more than just the apparent problems. Not all items noted will necessarily need immediate attention.

> Be prepared to get more than one type of survey. For instance, a worrying crack may be outside the remit of your surveyor and may require a structural engineer's report. Although this sounds expensive, far better to spend the money now getting good advice than regret the purchase later.

> Always use impartial consultants and never rely on free surveys; those who offer them may have a vested interest in selling a product.

> If specific work may need to be done, for instance re-thatching, do not be afraid to get quotations before you sign a contract.

> Beware of mortgage restrictions imposed by a lender which may insist on the use of modern materials or the installation of things such as damp-proof courses – such conditions can sometimes be lifted if backed by a good surveyor's report.

If you have doubts, be prepared to walk away. An old house, particularly one that needs work, is a major commitment that should not be entered into lightly.

Above: Taking on a wreck is not a job for the fainthearted; be sure to understand the implications fully before you buy.

Above: Some old buildings look far worse than they actually are. While this house in Norfolk has suffered serious neglect in recent years, a skilled joiner may well, for example, be able to repair the existing windows. Get a quotation before you put in an offer.

Above: The conversion of buildings that were not originally intended to be homes may not provide ideal living accommodation. It is important to consider whether a change of use will diminish their history and integrity; in the case of a mill, the loss of old machinery and internal divisions might be incurred.

Above right: Buildings like this one in the Orkney Isles that have been derelict for many years are often the most rewarding to repair; start by looking at what can be saved rather than what needs to be replaced.

only potentially harm and disfigure, they make it hard to see what really needs attention. Equally, buildings that have been severely neglected are frequently suffering from rot and decay because water has penetrated deep into the structure.

LISTING AND CONSERVATION AREAS

A key consideration when buying is whether the building is listed or lies within a conservation area, since this brings potential benefits, limitations and legal responsibilities. Listing is done to identify and protect our heritage and the list records a wide variety of structures, from castles and cathedrals to milestones and village pumps. Most owners are pleased that their houses are listed and it can add to their value.

Check with your solicitor whether a house is listed; never rely on the estate agent's details. Your local planning authority should be able to supply you with a copy of the list description which will give some information about the listing. Contrary to popular belief, buildings are listed in their entirety, even though some parts may be more important than others. Just because a particular feature is not mentioned within the description does not mean it is not legally protected. It is possible that elements such as garden walls and outbuildings will be covered by the listing of a house or listed separately.

If you wish to demolish, alter or extend a listed building in a way that affects its character, inside or out, you must apply for 'listed building consent'. This can be

required for such things as cleaning brickwork, painting or even replacing more recent additions such as modern windows. So, if in doubt, check before work starts, or you may find you have committed a criminal offence and be forced to undertake expensive remedial works.

The owners of listed buildings can be forced to make repairs if the condition becomes poor. The materials and details of alterations are likely to be controlled.

REPAIR NOT RESTORE

Changes and alterations over time add to a building's story, though this does not mean that damaging past mistakes cannot be put right. Ideas about what is worth saving change constantly – once all Victorian alterations to older buildings were automatically removed; now there is far greater thought for the overall evolution and history of the building.

Above: Over half of all listed buildings are houses, and they are more likely to be listed the older and rarer they are. Generally, buildings from before 1700 which survive in anything like their original condition are listed, as are most built between 1700 and 1840. From this period on, the criteria become tighter.

Right: As is clearly demonstrated here in Chiddingfold, Surrey, any building needs to be seen in the context of its setting. If one of a group is altered or inappropriately repaired, it is likely to devalue its neighbours aesthetically; this is one of the considerations when conservation areas are established.

Above: As with many old buildings, this house in Suffolk has evolved. It has been dramatically altered and added to many times in its history, the accretions telling the story of fashion, technology and function.

Right: As much as possible of the original fabric of this mud and stud building in Lincolnshire is being saved as it undergoes careful repair using only traditional techniques.

The general approach to building conservation was established in 1877 when William Morris founded The Society for the Protection of Ancient Buildings (SPAB). In its manifesto he set out a philosophy of repair rather than restoration which guides the Society's work to this day.

Repair is based on the principle of mending buildings with the minimum loss of fabric and, in so doing, keeping their character and authenticity. Contrary to this, 'restoration' means work intended to return an old building to a perfect state. In other words, putting things back to how they were, or how we think they were, rather than preserving them as they are now with all their wonderful scars of time and history. Restoration is generally highly destructive and, as Morris states in the manifesto, 'a feeble and lifeless forgery is the final result of all the wasted labour'.

Left: Try to keep the clues that tell the story of the past. This stone-mullioned window could easily be reconstructed, but the later nineteenth-century casement window is vital evidence of the building's evolution.

Below: An old building in the wrong hands can so easily be stripped of all the intangible elements that make it special. This building (top) was virtually dismantled (centre) and reconstructed (bottom) to produce a vague facsimile of its original form, yet it could easily have been repaired and its elements retained.

Putting the philosophy outlined by Morris into practice means, for example, repairing only the decayed bottom rail of an original sash window rather than the whole sash. The aim is not to hide imperfections such as bulges, bows, sags and leans but rather to respect them. When making repairs this means not artificially ageing new elements. For example, you would not stain a new oak beam but rather let it age naturally over time, so the history of the building is still clear. When repairs are made, new material should always be fitted to the old and not the old adapted to accept the new. In this way more ancient fabric will survive.

Even the best-maintained buildings cannot withstand decay or damage entirely; the goal is to avoid any unnecessary loss and, when any alterations or repairs are made, they should be capable of being understood and of being reversible in the future. For instance, if you decide to divide a room into two with a stud wall, do it so that there is minimum damage to the existing fabric by cutting the stud work round the existing cornice and skirting board rather than cutting through them to make way for the new partition.

Another consideration is the use of second-hand materials. Before going to a salvage yard to buy, think where the items may have come from. The use of architectural features from elsewhere confuses the understanding and appreciation of a building at a later date. Trade in salvaged materials encourages architectural theft, whereas demand for the same materials, but new, helps keep them in production. The use of different but compatible materials can be an honest alternative, and new work should be of its time. Indeed, good new architecture can sit happily alongside old and is preferable to ill-informed pastiche.

Right: Theft for architectural salvage can lead to the loss of important features. When items such as fireplaces are moved to houses to which they are unconnected, they will cause confusion to those trying to understand the history of the building in the future.

Below: Victorian and Edwardian houses are rich in history and an important part of our architectural heritage. The original features that we save now are the treasures of the future.

BE PROPERLY INFORMED

Buildings are often unwittingly damaged through lack of knowledge and misapprehension, so understanding your home, its history and its surroundings should be a priority and often proves to be much of the fun of ownership. Find out as much as you can about why the building was built, the way it was built, the materials used and how it might have been decorated, furnished and lived in. Your local history centre is a useful starting point, as are museums and buildings similar to or of the same period as yours. Neighbours, their homes and past owners are frequently a rich fund of knowledge. For broader information, books and magazines are useful resources while the internet is invaluable.

Thinking early on about the skills and materials you may need could save you money and, when it comes to finding the right advisers, builders and craftsmen, will help give you a clearer idea of whether they have a feel for the needs of the building.

With an old house, it is not always possible to know the extent of the undertaking until you begin. The work can also be expensive because of the need to source and use traditional materials and craftspeople, so do not underestimate the cost of completing the project. Work out what you can afford and, if you go ahead, prioritise the work. Few grants or tax breaks are available and some building societies are reluctant to lend against buildings in need of substantial work but it is worth persevering since there are specialist lenders.

Remember that, while it is natural to want to find out more, there is a real danger in stripping off things such as old plaster or removing fireplaces simply to discover what is underneath. It is potentially damaging to the building, will undoubtedly be expensive in the long run and may land you in trouble if the building is listed.

The conservation approach

Conservation is about respect and care and keeping as much of the original as possible. Things to think about when working on your house include:

> Conserve rather than restore, repair rather than replace.
> Retain the patina of age.
> Carry out honest repairs; don't artificially age new materials.
> Use tried and tested materials.
> Make additions reversible wherever possible.
> Respect historic alterations and additions.
> Don't try to put back what has been lost.
> Don't be afraid of good new design.
> Carry out regular maintenance.
> Bear in mind the words of William Morris: 'We are only trustees for those who come after us.'

Below: Careful and honest repair – in this case to a window in a timber-framed house – rather than wholesale replacement is an essential tenet of conservation. It retains as much of the original fabric and history of the building as possible.

Below: Be careful not to lose original fabric in your eagerness to get the project under way. Here, vestiges of ancient plaster and original floorboards remain within the fourteenth-century building; they could be incorporated when repairs are undertaken.

Advice from the experts

Above: Practical courses are by far the best way of getting to grips with repair work; for example, hands-on traditional plastering brings an immediate understanding of the materials and techniques involved.

The best way to learn about your old house is to take part in a specialist course. Among the organisations offering such training is The Society for the Protection of Ancient Buildings (SPAB).

The SPAB runs courses and events to provide homeowners with the knowledge necessary to make informed decisions about the repair of their houses, and has a range of publications which are highly respected for giving authoritative and practical guidance on the repair and care of buildings. The SPAB is able to supply advice over the telephone as well as details of specialist craftspeople, architects, building surveyors and other professionals.

GETTING INTIMATE

Be aware how easy it is to destroy hundreds of years of history in minutes. It is sometimes said that all the best things in a building go into the skip in the first week.

Obviously, making your home watertight and secure is a priority and must be done, even if only temporarily. From then on, remember that haste often produces mistakes that you may regret, while using the wrong materials or techniques can leave a mark as indelible as spilt red wine on a white tablecloth. Living with a building will help to make any work you do more appropriate to the way you intend to use it and more sympathetic to its needs.

Move slowly and you will find clues about the way the building was constructed and developed, and its past and present problems. Understand the spaces, the cupboards, the loft, the cellar; observe where the water collects when it rains, which rooms are filled by early-morning sun and which feel particularly bleak or damp in winter. In thinking about your house, never forget the importance of its setting and any garden walls, outbuildings or features which contribute to its overall context.

Your ideas will change and evolve and will influence not just any alterations you may make to the structure but the way in which you eventually decorate. Always think how any work you do will affect the building and, when you do start work, always try to repair rather than replace – after all, the building is only authentic if original parts remain.

Poverty is often said to be the best preserver of old buildings. While not altogether true, it is certainly the case that most irreparable damage or loss is the result of poorly informed repair or over-zealous alterations.

Above: After you have made your house watertight and propped its ailing bones, make time to think through the next stages. Better to delay and get it right than to regret a decision made in haste.

Above: Without the will or expertise, many wonderful features are lost. This 200-year-old ceiling could easily be replaced with angular plasterboard, but the charm of the room would vanish.

Getting the work done

Whether you employ professionals or do it yourself, building work is rarely straightforward and almost always takes longer and costs more than you originally expect. Even so, repairing a building sympathetically and making it your home can be hugely rewarding.

The scale and complexity of work will vary considerably from one building to another. At the outset, you must decide how much you are prepared to take on yourself. Are you getting plans drawn up or can you manage without? Will an architect run the project or will you oversee the works? Are you taking on a main contractor or individual tradesmen? The route you take should be dependent on your own level of experience and available time. It is critical to get professional advice where it is needed, and this could even save you money on a complex job.

Whoever you employ will need to be properly briefed by you, so it is useful to have a good understanding of the processes involved. If you are going to manage the work yourself you will need to be fully immersed in the project. Understanding the building, research, thorough planning, tackling tasks in the right order, patience, realistic budgeting and finding the right team of people to work on your project are all essential elements of success. Perhaps the most important single piece of advice is not to underestimate the amount of your time you will need to devote every day.

PROFESSIONAL ADVISERS

If you are contemplating work of any scale or complexity you are likely to require the services of a building surveyor, architect or structural engineer. Never underestimate the pitfalls of old building repairs and alterations: trying to do without professional advice can be a big mistake, particularly if you have inadequate experience.

Always employ people who understand and are sympathetic to old buildings. Interview them, and make sure they share the same 'philosophy of repair'; this is more important than anything else. Inspect their completed work, talk to their clients and ensure that they carry professional indemnity insurance.

Opposite: Whether you are repairing a Victorian London terrace, such as here, or an ancient rural cottage, thorough planning and careful management apply in equal measure.

Above: Decisions taken early on about how the work is to be undertaken and managed will be crucial to the overall success of the project in terms of time-scale, cost, quality of work and the integrity of the building.

A good building professional will help you resolve problems while maintaining the integrity of the building. He or she will also understand legislation and may have an existing rapport with your conservation officer. A good architect, surveyor or engineer will know what information needs to be submitted, and will produce plans that are likely to help you achieve the necessary consents without repeated applications and wasted time. An architect may be appointed just to produce the plans or details of the work, or can be retained to manage the project through to completion.

Never be afraid of questioning professional advisers and scrutinise carefully any plans and specifications they produce. Ask about the cost implications of adding or removing elements, and ensure that top-grade materials are specified. It is your home and it should meet your needs and aspirations, not just your architect's!

Should you intend to alter or extend your home you will probably need approval. If so, do not under any circumstances begin without confirmation in writing. Listed building consent may be required, but you should also be aware of Building Control and planning permission. These are invariably administered by different people within your local authority.

In conservation areas, registered parks and gardens, national parks, areas of outstanding natural beauty and the Norfolk and Suffolk Broads, you may need planning permission or consent for work that would not be required in other areas.

Building inspectors, planners and conservation officers can be flexible when it comes to reconciling modern building regulations with sympathetic repairs and alterations, so suggest to them what you would like to do and ask their advice and what the limits would be, rather than provide them immediately with a *fait accompli*. Throughout any project it is well worth attending site meetings with local authority staff to ensure that you are aware of any issues as and when they occur.

Architects, surveyors and some contractors will understand the necessary procedures and should draw up the relevant plans and documentation. They will also make any necessary applications for you, but never assume that your builder knows the law. A fee has to be paid for planning permission and approval under building regulations, but there is no charge for listed building consent. When the work is finished, get it signed off by Building Control and ensure that any planning or listing conditions have been formally discharged; keep all permissions and plans – you will need them if you sell your home.

Work to your property may also involve you in some slightly more unusual aspects of the law. For example, even if you do not know they are there, bat roosts are legally protected: always consult the relevant authorities if you have any doubts. Another consideration is archaeology, especially when digging footings or trenches for drains. Occasionally, a site or structure will be a scheduled monument and will need special consent for any excavation, alteration or repair.

Top tip: Priorities

The most necessary work is not always the most exciting or rewarding. With any building, the first priority is to ensure that it is watertight, otherwise decay will set in and unnecessary destruction of the fabric will occur. Always spend your time and money on the essentials first.

Left: Erecting a temporary roof not only helps by providing immediate protection to the building; it also means that work can continue in bad weather.

source of information and will need to become involved if you intend to undertake major repairs or alterations.

As work progresses, keep the conservation officer informed and, if you do not agree with what is being suggested, clearly state your case. If what is being asked for has major cost implications, point this out. Equally, officers can be helpful in bringing your builders into line when it comes to issues of conservation.

Listed building application forms now usually ask for a 'Design and Access Statement' to accompany your plans. This is an explanation of what is proposed, why it is considered necessary and what impact it is likely to have on the building's historic significance. It is an opportunity to set out your case in writing and show that the changes have been properly considered. If your application is unsuccessful there is a right of appeal.

Listed building consent

Listed building consent from the local planning authority is required for listed buildings in addition to any planning permission. Consent is required for any demolition and any alteration, inside or out, that affects the character of a listed building. Repairs with like-for-like materials do not usually require consent; however, this is rather a grey area and your local authority conservation officer will advise on whether an application is necessary. Do not assume that, just because a feature is not mentioned in the listing description, it is not covered by the legislation: a listed building is protected in its entirety. Structures in a listed building's 'curtilage' – the land around it – may be covered by the listing, too.

The idea of submitting a listed building application may seem daunting, but in fact the majority of applications are approved, particularly when they are carefully thought through. It is worth being honest from the start, as a conservation officer can often prove to be a useful

Right: Even in its derelict state, the historic significance of this fourteenth-century building in Somerset is clearly apparent. Any further work will require listed building consent to ensure the maximum survival of its remaining features such as the roof structure, panelling, door and floors.

Applying for listed building consent

For minor matters it is relatively easy to make your own application for listed building consent. Details of how to apply should be available from your local planning office. You are likely to need scale drawings showing the extent of the proposed works – an architectural draughtsman should be able to carry these out if you do not have an architect or surveyor involved. For the simplest application, annotated photographs may suffice.

Listed building consent is free, and any alterations for which consent has been granted may be zero-rated for VAT. For instance, the cost of the VAT (if your contractor is VAT-registered) might be saved on a new central heating system if it was granted consent.

Planning permission

Planning permission is separate from listed building consent and other controls. There is no simple definition of when planning permission may be needed. For example, loft conversions generally do not require it (though they would probably need listed building consent), but installing a tank to store liquefied petroleum gas does. Normally, the concern is more with external alterations than internal ones, but dividing a property into separate units or changing its use will require permission. In conservation areas, certain changes come under 'permitted development' but some extra controls exist; permitted development rights are also reduced for any listed building.

As with building control, an application is made to your local planning department. Ask whether there are likely to be any difficulties which could be overcome by amending the proposal. Occasionally, if you wish to see what the council thinks of your ideas, you can make an outline application. These are possible only with planning permission, not with listed building or conservation area consent.

Building control

Approval may be needed for both new works and alterations. Building control is concerned with standards and safety, and deals with materials and methods of construction.

You apply by contacting the building control officer at your local council. Once work begins, you must inform them before certain stages are started so that inspections can be made to ensure compliance with the regulations. Be sure that these are carried out; otherwise you may find that you have to undo work to prove that things have been done properly. Where possible, attend site meetings. At the end of the job, ensure that the building control officer undertakes a final inspection and grants his approval in writing before you pay the builder's final bill.

Future changes

Building legislation of all kinds changes regularly. Before proceeding, check with the local planning authority that your understanding of controls is up to date.

BUILDERS

The success or failure of your project rests largely with your builders and tradesmen. If you are managing the work yourself, you will be dealing with them on a daily basis and greatly dependent on their advice and experience, so it is critical to nurture a good working relation-

Left: Before doing any work that may require approval under the Building Regulations, ensure that you have followed the correct procedures, otherwise you may be required to open up certain works to allow the building control officer access for inspection.

Left: If you are attached to a neighbouring property and are planning to carry out works to the wall dividing the two houses, you may be subject to party wall legislation. A surveyor specialising in party wall works should be consulted.

ship. It is likely that the best builders will be booked up weeks or months in advance but it is better to wait than compromise.

DOCUMENTATION
Schedules and specifications

For simpler projects, a schedule of works may be all that is required. This is a list of items against which the contractor is asked to price. It is often accompanied by a drawing or plan in diagrammatic form – for instance, indicating where drainage runs are to be laid. Depending on your experience, you may be able to organise this information yourself.

For more complex projects, scale drawings and a specification may be required. This is a more detailed description of the works and includes a section on materials and craftsmanship. It is usually prepared by a professional advisor.

It is important that these documents are precise and unambiguous. Avoid using words such as 'overhaul', 'refurbish', 'repair' or 'make good as required'. For

Top tip: Choosing your builder

Try to judge whether your potential builders have a feeling for old buildings and the 'philosophy of repair':

> Do they use pure lime mixes with no cement?
> Are they happy to repair an old window rather than replace it?
> Do they think an old wall will work without the installation of a damp-proof course?
> Do they get on with conservation officers?

If the answer is 'no' to any of these questions, they probably are not suitable.

Below: As well as finding someone who has experience in the task in hand, it is important to choose a builder whom you like and trust.

Builder checklist

> Always give your builder a written document to price against.
> Get at least three written quotations, not estimates. Ensure that they are itemised so that you can take an item out at a later stage
> If elements of the works are unresolved, ask the builder to include a provisional sum in his quotation but try to keep these works to a minimum.

> Ensure that the price includes clearing all building rubbish from the site.
> If your builder is VAT-registered, check if VAT is included in the quotation.
> Request references that you can follow up, then go and see at least two examples of past work and try to speak to the builder's client alone. The work should preferably involve a similar type and age of building to your own.
> When comparing quotations, look for hidden extras and do not necessarily choose the lowest price.
> If a builder says he belongs to a professional body, check that this is true.
> Agree all stage payments before work starts, and never pay 'up front'.
> Avoid anyone who 'prefers cash'.
> Even apparently reputable firms may not always do the work themselves. Check if they are planning to use subcontractors, since their work may not be to the same standard.
> Ensure that all contractors have full public liability insurance and employers' liability cover; ask to see the relevant certificates.
> Check who is liable for materials and machinery while on site.
> If possible protect yourself against faulty workmanship and materials by ensuring that contractors have insurance-backed warranties which cover their work even if they go out of business.
> Remember that most builders are not designers but enablers – the design work is the responsibility of you or your architect.
> Be sure you know what you want, otherwise there are likely to be problems at some point during the project.

Left: The right builder will ultimately determine the success or failure of your project. Be prepared to wait until he has a slot in his schedule.

Right: The value of good builders should never be underrated. Even so, this example of work in progress is not advisable practice from the point of view of health and safety!

example, instead of putting 'paint windows', specify the paint system to be used including the method of preparation, the number of coats to be applied, the make of paint, and the colour and finish required.

Although this process is time-consuming, it should allow quotations from different builders to be compared 'like for like': they will all be quoting for identical work, products and materials, rather than making their own judgement on what they think you want. It also means that you have a document to refer to should there be any dispute in the future.

Contracts

All of these documents will form part of the contract with the contractors you employ. The simplest way of implementing a contract is an exchange of letters. Included should be the agreed price, payment terms, start and finish dates and any warranty.

Where large sums are involved, it is worth employing a professional advisor to draw up the contract to protect your legal position. If you are managing the works yourself, simplified contract documents are available for a modest charge from the Joint Contracts Tribunal (JCT), aimed at an assortment of different-sized projects. Free contracts are available from the Federation of Master Builders.

Above: Careful documentation helps prevent ambiguities and ensures that everyone involved is working to the same specification, thus making it easier to compare prices and resolve possible disputes.

Right: Exploratory 'opening up' prior to works starting on site may give a clearer idea of what is going to be involved. Even so, it may not reveal all the problems, so it is important to agree a rate for extras with your builder.

Top tip: The golden rule of cost control

Changing your mind is expensive! Try to design as much of the work as possible before you get your quotation, even if this causes a delay to the start. When builders are pricing for a job, they will be competitive and will give you the best price. If you change your mind once they have started on site, they will be able to charge whatever they wish and you will have no comeback. Some unscrupulous builders will put in a low price for a poorly detailed specification in the knowledge that they will make their profits in the extras.

Changes and extras

When dealing with old buildings it is often hard for you or the builder to know exactly what will be involved until work begins and some exploratory 'opening up' has been undertaken. Consequently, you must agree hourly or daily rates and how extra materials may be charged so that a fair price can be agreed between both parties at a later stage.

Although it is rare to undertake any building work without making changes along the way, try to keep them to a minimum and be disciplined, particularly at the start of a project. Alterations to the planned scope of works are known as 'extras': they inevitably cost money and disrupt schedules, and can also require the undoing of work that has already been competed. It is important to

agree the cost involved before any extra work is undertaken, since even seemingly small changes can cost significant sums. Confirm all instructions, however minor, with your advisors or builders formally in writing. Equally, agree any cost reductions during the build.

THE BUILD

For neighbours the prospect of building work can be worrying, so keep them informed of what is happening. By showing them plans early you can reassure them; providing what you propose is reasonable, they are less likely to object if you make a planning application. In addition, they will probably be more tolerant of mess and noise if they know how long it will go on and what is causing it. They will also help with security by keeping an eye on the property when you are not around.

Preparing the site

Like a patient on an operating table, buildings are most at risk when the work begins. Protection works should be carried out before your builder starts or be built in to the specification as part of the contract:

> Building sites, materials and tools are vulnerable to vandalism, theft and even arson. Install temporary fencing, gates and intruder alarms where necessary.
> Protect the building from accidental damage before and during work, especially if it is unoccupied. Windows and doors should be shielded externally and internally with timber boarding or heavy-gauge plastic sheeting.
> Architectural details such as fireplaces and staircases should temporarily be covered with boarding to prevent damage and to screen them from the eyes of thieves.
> Protect floors with sheets of plywood or hardboard, gaffer-taped at the joints. Schedule work to avoid floors being lifted repeatedly by different trades when services are being installed.
> If scaffolding is being erected, care needs to be taken to ensure that windows with original glass are not broken and that other detailing is not chipped.
> At no point during work leave your building without rainwater goods – temporary plastic gutters are ideal.
> Take precautions against fire from the start. Place fire extinguishers and sand buckets at strategic points, have a water supply and hose to hand and install temporary battery-operated smoke alarms during

Right: Before embarking on any work check that your building is properly protected and the site meets all the requirements in terms of public liability, especially when it is beside a highway.

Below: Protecting surfaces such as floors is relatively easy but should be carried out before any work starts on site.

Bottom: Securing the building from intruders and protecting windows and other features from damage should be undertaken at the earliest opportunity.

work to provide early warning. Never allow smoking in or around the building. Stop any 'hot works' such as the use of blowtorches and angle grinders at least one hour before leaving the site, and make sure the area is thoroughly checked before locking up.

Managing the build

At the outset, walk round the building with your tradesmen; tell them something about its history, point out the features that are important and ask them to let you know immediately if they discover anything interesting – for example, traces of old wallpaper, letters or coins in voids.

Record-keeping is an essential element of any building project if you are to get the result you want and bring it in on budget. Keep a diary and take photographs before any work starts and at every stage along the way. Record all bills that are paid, who is on site each day, the materials delivered and any events that stop work, such as adverse weather. Maintain detailed records of all site meetings: these become invaluable if there are any disputes further down the line.

Bear in mind that building work invariably takes longer than anyone expects, including the builders

Left: Building works are likely to uncover items from the past. Brief your tradesmen from the outset and ask them to report any such discoveries.

themselves. It may sometimes seem haphazard, but good builders will be working along a logical path so that the different trades are on site at the right time and the minimum time is wasted. Two essential stages are 'first fix' and 'second fix'. First fix involves the installation of elements such as pipework, electrical cables and socket boxes; second fix is when everything is connected up and the socket fronts and taps are put on.

For major projects, it is generally better for everyone concerned if you move out rather than try to survive in one or two rooms. Where this is not practical, agree working hours with the contractor, keep work areas clear of your belongings, children and pets, and be adaptable so that the work can proceed safely and in a sensible order.

If at any time you are not satisfied with the quality of the work or there are indications that things are going wrong, act immediately and talk through the issues with the builder or your advisors.

Towards the end of the project, draw up a snagging list and go through the items on it with the builder. Always hold money back until all issues have been rectified; under a standard contract, 5 per cent is customary.

MATERIALS

Never underestimate the time it can take to select materials and products. With old buildings, matching and sourcing items such as bricks can be hugely time-consuming but is often crucial to a successful end result. Even with items such as taps and sanitary ware, getting the look you want will usually take longer than you expect; if the contractor needs the item, there is a danger

Protecting your investment

> Do all that you can to ensure that those working on site gain respect for the building and understand the 'philosophy of repair'.
> Instil a 'like-for-like' repair methodology.
> Avoid the use of modern methods simply because the alternatives are unfamiliar or are difficult to purchase locally.
> Always listen to the views of your advisors and builders, but never be afraid to challenge what they are doing and never make assumptions that they know best.
> If you have done your research, you may even be able to pass on valuable knowledge.
> Always intervene if you feel the integrity of the building is being put at risk.

Right: However many tradesmen and professionals are involved, remember it is your house and you have a key role to play in ensuring a successful outcome. Listen to the advice of others but be prepared to carry out your own research and take an active role throughout the project.

that you may be pushed into a decision you will later regret.

> If you are working on a big project and buying the materials yourself, set up an account with your local builders' merchant. This should save you money because discounts are usually offered.
> When you are buying materials for a contractor, make sure you agree in advance that they are suitable for purpose, otherwise the materials (and you) may be blamed for problems.
> Order all goods well in advance and check delivery times and costs – delays on site will be expensive.
> When arranging delivery of heavy materials, ask whether the vehicle has a crane and plan in advance how it will be unloaded.
> Do not pay the contractor for any materials until they are on site.

> Unless they are appropriate to the building, avoid getting carried away with embellishments such as flamboyant hopper heads, twee 'carriage lamps' and cast iron nameplates.
> Beware of 'miracle' products!

MONEY MATTERS

Careful management of the financial aspects of any building project is crucial, even more so when the work is extensive and spread over a long period. This is particularly important where mortgage-providers withhold some funds and make payments only as certain stages are completed. Although grants are now rare, if you think you may be eligible apply in good time and do not start work before you have the grant.

Work to old buildings is invariably unpredictable and presents unexpected problems which can wreak havoc

Above: Think in advance about how deliveries will be made. Is there suitable access? Are parked cars going to be in the way? Will power or telephone lines prevent the use of a crane?

Scaffolding

Wherever possible, scaffolding should be arranged by your builder but it is worth being aware of certain points:

> Make sure a reputable firm is used which carries insurance.
> Ensure that a handing-over certificate has been issued by the scaffolder before anyone uses the scaffold. It must then be inspected by a competent person before use, every week and after damage or alteration.
> If work is being undertaking to outside walls, the scaffold may need to be set back slightly from the wall's surface for access.
> Ensure that scaffolders use protective end-caps on scaffold poles.
> If roof tiles are likely to be broken when dismantling scaffolding, have spares ready and ask the scaffolder to replace them.
> When re-roofing, it may be worth erecting a temporary roof over the building for protection and to allow work to continue in bad weather.

Right: Scaffolding must always be erected by insured and licensed contractors. It is costly, so plan carefully to take full advantage of the access it provides while in place.

with even the best-laid plans. Allow for a contingency fund of not less than 20 per cent and be ready to remove non-essential items from later stages of the project if you look like going over budget.

Agree payment terms with all contractors before work commences, and ensure they are set out in the contract. On larger projects, it is common to pay for work on completion of each stage. Alternatively, ask the builder to submit monthly invoices and include an estimated final account with each so as not to lose track of the budget.

Beware of making any payments in advance: you may never see your money or the builder again! As work nears completion, make a snagging list of all the things that still have to be done and submit this in writing. Do not settle the final account until all items have been completed.

Above: Adequate insurance on any house is essential. Buildings are most at risk while work is in progress, so make your insurance company aware of your plans.

INSURANCE

Old buildings tend to be more expensive to repair than modern ones. With listed buildings, in particular, it is vital that you have adequate insurance. If the worst happens, you may be legally obliged to match not only existing detail and construction techniques but also the materials originally employed.

A number of companies offer special insurances for thatched, historic and unusual properties. These companies should have the advantage of understanding the risks and legal implications and be more sympathetic to preserving the original features of the building in the event of a claim.

> Check to make sure you can get cover before you buy the property.
> Always tell your insurers you are having building work done or if the building will be unoccupied.
> Advise your insurers of the increasing value of the house as it is worked on, and that you may need cover for materials, tools and equipment on site.
> Give as much information as possible and disclose all relevant facts, otherwise you may breach the contract.
> An under-insured value will generally result in the imposition of an 'average' clause, which may leave you out of pocket.

> Record the building, outbuildings and garden in case of fire, theft or vandalism. Take photographs and have plans, drawings and descriptions of the building; pay particular attention to unusual features and architectural details such as fireplaces, doors and ironmongery. Keep this information somewhere secure – preferably off site.

HEALTH AND SAFETY

Building sites are dangerous places; in your enthusiasm, never forget to give thought to your safety and that of others. Old buildings can pose extra dangers – they may be unstable or have faulty electrical systems or even poorly maintained gas supplies.

Until its harmful effects were realised, asbestos was used widely in all types of buildings because of its fire-resistance and thermal properties; it is also found in some textured wall finishes. It is a risk to health only if asbestos fibres are released into the air and breathed in. If you discover asbestos, leave well alone and consult your local authority about the procedures for dealing with it.

Lead is also found in many old buildings: in paint, lead water pipes and, until more recently, the solder used for copper water pipes so you may wish to have your drinking water tested for lead content (➡ Safety first, page 167).

Top tip: Recording for the future

We are just temporary guardians of old houses. It is essential to keep details of all the work you carry out: just as you have enjoyed finding records of the past, so will the homeowner of the future. Try to keep hard copies relating to what you have done and print photographs rather than rely on digital information. This will allow owners who follow you to make informed decisions as well as provide historical understanding.

Left: Health and safety has become a key issue. Check that your contractors are fully insured and take care to fulfil any responsibilities you may have as the client.

Safety check list

> Buy a first aid kit and keep it on site. Eye wash and eye bath are essential.
> Always equip yourself properly for whatever job you are doing. Wear protective clothing, goggles, mask, gloves, sturdy footwear and hard hat. Avoid clothing that may catch in machinery.
> Ensure that ladders, access towers, scaffolding and temporary protection for the work are secure and suitable for the job.
> Many building materials are deceptively heavy or may be awkward to manoeuvre, so get help with lifting particularly when working at height.
> Always have a mobile phone with you.
> Try to avoid working alone. If you do work alone, tell someone and arrange to be in touch with them at prearranged times.
> Build bonfires well away from buildings, never leave them unattended and never have a bonfire near a thatched property.
> Cooperate with contractors and ensure that they are doing everything possible to minimise health and safety risks, noise and pollution. All those working on your property who are 'at work', such as trades- or craftspeople, are subject to the Health and Safety at Work Act.

3

Breathability and damp

In recent decades, damp walls have often been treated using sealants and cement-based products in a misguided attempt to keep water out. In fact, this is the worst possible approach since it locks dampness in. Instead, permeable materials should be used, since these allow the wall to breathe.

The way old buildings work is incredibly simple. Before the days of cavity walls, structures had 'solid' walls built of breathable materials. Where bricks and stones were used, they were generally bonded with weak and permeable mortars made of lime and sand. The external walls were often coated with a lime render which was limewashed so the structure was able to 'breathe'. When it rained, moisture was absorbed a few millimetres into the external surface but was able to evaporate as soon as the rain stopped, helped by the drying effects of the sun and wind.

Inside, walls were plastered with lime and finished with simple breathable paints. Any excess internal humidity from washing, cooking and human activity was dispersed via open flues and draughts, or absorbed by breathable surfaces. In addition, a kitchen range or open fire burnt from autumn until spring, drawing air through the home and keeping internal surfaces at a steady temperature. Provided the building was maintained, the structure remained essentially dry.

A change started to occur in the second half of the nineteenth century as new building methods began to be introduced. The interwar period saw many experi-

mental building types and, by the late 1940s, lime was largely replaced by cement. Modern building technology is the exact opposite of traditional solid, breathing walls. It relies on impervious outer layers, cavity walls and barriers against moisture.

Opposite: Traditional buildings are the antithesis of their modern equivalents; they were built with permeable materials that allow them to breathe. It is these very qualities that enable buildings such as this stone farmhouse in Wiltshire to develop a beautiful surface patina.

Right: There is nothing mysterious about the way solid walls are constructed, allowing a building to breathe. Here, the permeable mortar used to bond the stones can clearly be seen while the internal face was finished in a lime plaster.

Material conflict

Both traditional and modern methods of building are able to function efficiently if they are done well and are properly detailed. But over the last four decades, as the understanding of traditional solid walls has largely disappeared, builders have tried to apply modern techniques to breathing structures. Cement renders, along with 'plastic' paints, waterproof sealants and damp-proof courses, act as barriers to the wall's natural ability to breathe. This is when trouble occurs, with a mix of technologies that trap water within permeable materials, exacerbating the very problems that they are trying to resolve.

Right: The problems resulting from the use of cement render on an old building are all too clear to see. The impermeable render is trapping moisture, resulting in damp and structural failure.

Below: Breathing building. The walls of traditional buildings absorb moisture but this readily evaporates, leaving the structure dry. There are no impermeable barriers to trap moisture at any point.

Below: Modern cavity wall. Modern cavity walls work on an entirely different principle from the breathing wall; they are designed to block moisture transfer at every junction and every surface.

Below: Solid wall with modern materials applied. Problems arise when the two technologies are combined and impermeable materials are inappropriately applied to hitherto breathing walls.

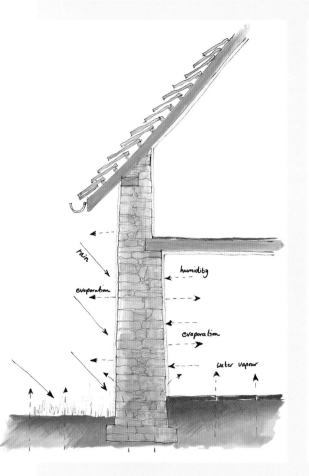

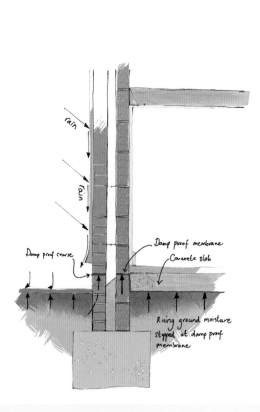

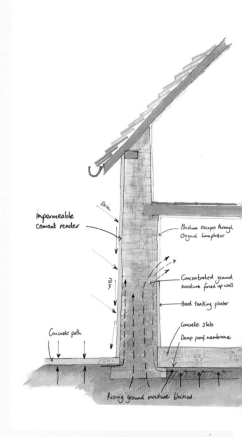

DEALING WITH DAMP

Virtually everyone living in an old house will experience some sort of 'damp problem', varying from something simple that is easily remedied to a longstanding issue that is impossible to resolve and may have to be 'managed' and accepted. The most important rule is to diagnose the true cause and, if possible, tackle the problem at source, rather than simply treat the symptoms.

Damp can be classified in five basic categories.

1. Condensation

This is due to excess humidity or 'water vapour' within a room, condensing on a cold surface. If this is a regular occurrence, black spots of mould will form. Condensation is a particular problem in steamy kitchens and bathrooms but also in cold corners on outside walls where ventilation is poor, such as behind wardrobes. It is usually resolved by improving ventilation, either by mechanical means with extraction fans or simply by opening windows regularly. Improving insulation to create warmer surfaces may also reduce the effect of condensation, for example by laying insulation above affected ceilings. Care needs to be taken when insulating walls that condensation does not form within the wall itself; this is known as interstitial condensation.

Right: Damp can be hugely damaging if left unchecked, but it is vital to make certain that you have rectified the original defect before treating the symptoms.

Above far right: Black spots of mould are indicative of condensation, though this is regularly misdiagnosed. Improved ventilation and insulation will usually resolve the problem.

2. Penetrating or lateral damp

This is damp that tracks across from the outside surface to the inside, usually due to a building defect. It may be due to a leaky gutter or downpipe, a rotten windowsill or defective pointing which, over a period of time, allows moisture through the wall. Such defects are usually easy to spot and straightforward to address. Penetrating damp may also cause damp ingress at the base of a wall if the external ground is higher than the internal floor level.

3. Rising damp

Before the mid nineteenth century, physical damp-proof courses (DPCs) were very rare. Many solid walled structures continued to be built without them well into the twentieth century. Early DPCs consisted of a course of slate built into the base of the wall. Later, a double course of engineering bricks or a layer of bitumen was used to resist rising moisture. DPCs became mandatory under the Public Health Act of 1875. This ushered in a

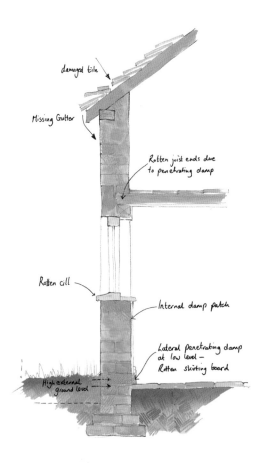

damaged tile

Missing Gutter

Rotten joist ends due to penetrating damp

Rotten cill

Internal damp patch

Lateral penetrating damp at low level – Rotten skirting board

High external ground level

Left: Penetrating damp is the result of any building defect that allows moisture to track through the external shell to the internal environment. Such defects can usually be readily corrected if the cause is identified.

Below: Early damp-proof courses generally consisted of a layer of slate at low level. Where these exist, they continue to function unless they have been damaged or breached.

Bottom: Gravel alongside a wall creates an evaporation zone, allowing water to escape from the base and minimising or even eliminating the effects of rising damp. In this case, the ground has been lowered around the external walls without reducing the level of the garden.

new approach to building which provided a belt-and-braces defence against rising damp, but millions of old houses continue to exist without DPCs and have no problem.

Generally speaking, there are two principal causes of rising damp. First, if the base of the wall is sitting in excessively wet conditions, for example where there is a high water table or a leaking drain, moisture is drawn up via capillary action. By draining the soil or fixing the leak, these effects can be minimised. Secondly, if hard impermeable surfaces butt up against the wall either side, for instance a tarmac path externally or a concrete slab internally, any excess moisture beneath may be forced upwards via the only porous route. By providing evaporation zones either side of the wall, the problem will be alleviated.

High external ground levels or external building defects are often the cause of rising damp and can generally be easily remedied.

A common solution is to inject a silicone DPC into the base of the wall, but this is rarely effective. Injected DPCs work on the premise of forming a continuous, horizontal, impermeable barrier to moisture. In reality,

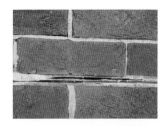

French drains

'French' or land drains are particularly useful for tackling waterlogged ground and for intercepting flows of excessive groundwater. They consist of a perforated pipe laid in a trench backfilled with pea shingle. As groundwater runs over the surface it percolates down through the shingle and is carried away by the pipe, either to a soakaway or to the surface water drain.

First, to avoid the pipe silting up, it is good practice to wrap it in a geotextile material which acts rather like a paper filter in a coffee machine.

Secondly, always design a French drain with 'rodding eyes' so it can be cleared by rodding or washing through with jets of water.

Be particularly cautious when digging a French drain near to the base of an old wall. Dig a trial hole first to establish the depth of your footing and soil conditions. The trench should generally be dug a minimum of half a metre from the house; always consult a surveyor or structural engineer if you have any cause for concern.

Below: A French drain is a means of addressing low level damp in areas of high water table, waterlogged ground or sloping sites.

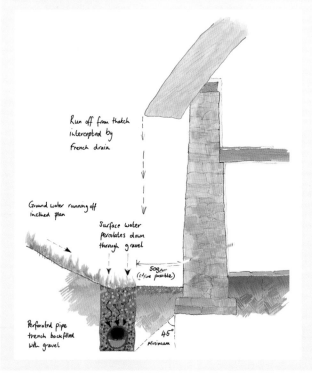

Run off from thatch intercepted by French drain

Ground water running off inclined plan

Surface water percolates down through gravel

Perforated pipe trench backfilled with gravel

50cm (if possible)

45° Minimum

Right: Buildings rarely had damp-proof courses before the mid-nineteenth century but their design took this into account. Never assume that a house without a DPC needs one.

Right: This is a blatant example of an unnecessarily injected damp-proof course. It is highly unlikely that this house has a rising damp problem, There is already a good damp-proof course provided by the engineering bricks; the internal floor level will be above this, and the external ground level is well below. The injected damp-proof course has in any case been applied into engineering bricks, which are too hard to allow the silicone to 'spread'. Unnecessary and visually catastrophic cement repointing has been carried out as part of the 'rising damp remedial works', probably to comply with the guarantee.

Below: The disastrous effects of applying a hard tanking plaster are clearly illustrated by the patch of damp on the more permeable plaster directly above it, where trapped moisture is emerging.

this is almost impossible to achieve through anything other than a physical DPC, such as traditional slate or modern plastic. In houses where there is no DPC, mortgage companies often insist on silicone injection, even when no signs of rising damp exist. This unnecessary work can, ironically, reduce the value of a property due to irreparable scarring and physical damage.

In order to qualify for a guarantee, injected DPCs are usually carried out in conjunction with hacking off internal plaster, regardless of its historic significance, to a metre high. This is replaced with a very hard tanking plaster, trapping residual dampness within the wall and preventing it from drying out.

Some companies specialise in cutting through the base of a wall in order to insert a physical DPC, but this is highly inadvisable due to the structural problems that can result.

Further problems can also be caused when rising damp is misdiagnosed, which is in a majority of cases.

4. Hygroscopic salts

Old buildings often contain areas of salt-laden plaster or masonry. This may be due to the use of salty unwashed sand for the original mortars or plasters, rising ground salts, salts from a marine environment or a variety of other causes. Mysterious salt patches can appear up to around a metre high on walls due to urine saturation in buildings where animals have been kept; they are also common on chimney breasts due to salts from flue gases.

Some of these salts are 'hygroscopic', meaning that they absorb moisture. In a humid environment, the wall

Top tip: Dealing with low level damp

> Establish the cause: get a drainage survey, check relative ground levels, check the condition of your external wall, check for leaking water and heating pipes.
> If you are on a slope, consider installing a French drain to intercept excessive rainwater.
> Encourage the wall to dry out: cut back any plants which are growing against the wall and, where possible, remove cement pointing/render externally and strip modern plaster finishes internally (➡ Preparing brickwork for repointing, page 47).
> If feasible, provide evaporation zones at the base of the wall by cutting away any tarmac or concrete externally that runs right up to the wall and replace it with gravel.
> Once walls have dried out, make good the surfaces using lime plaster/pointing and breathable paints.

Above: If soil or debris builds up against an external wall, it will cause penetrating damp at low level. This is often mistaken for rising damp, but can easily be rectified by clearing it away and allowing the wall to dry out.

may appear damp due to the salts temporarily holding this moisture. While residual salts cause little damage, they may be unsightly if they appear as damp patches. There is not much that can be done other than replacing the patch of plaster with new lime plaster; even this may not cure the problem if the walls are heavily salt-laden.

Salts appearing on the surface as white crystals should be dry brushed or vacuumed off; never try to wash them as they will be dissolved and reabsorbed into the wall.

5. Plumbing leaks

It is surprising how often plumbing leaks are ignored, hidden or misdiagnosed. Common problem areas include:

> The outlet at the back of a toilet pan, which may develop a minute leak over time but can go on to rot floorboards and joists in this rarely checked area.

> Copper pipes, which can develop pinhole leaks due to corrosion, wreaking havoc if not identified.

> Poor seals around shower trays, a frequent trouble spot, may go unnoticed for long periods, leading to an outbreak of rot under the tray or within stud walls.

Ideally, when installing a new plumbing system, access doors should be provided wherever possible so that vulnerable areas can be checked and fixed if necessary.

Left: Hygroscopic salts within the fabric attract moisture vapour from the internal environment and may appear as damp patches. They are commonly misdiagnosed and can be difficult to rectify, but are usually only superficial.

Resolving damp problems

Damp is the single biggest threat to old buildings. Once it has been identified and resolved, the next stage is to dry out the affected area. For a nine-inch brick wall, this can easily take six months. For a thick rubble stone wall, it may take years. Drying conditions can be improved by clearing vegetation externally and maximising air circulation. Internally, de-humidifiers may provide some assistance, provided the space is sealed off from the external environment. However, beware of over-drying joinery and causing shrinkage and cracking – it is better to open windows to create a through draught for ventilation and to provide heating to the area during cooler months.

Alternative solutions

Various remedies on the market claim to resolve low level damp. These include ceramic tubes set in the base of a wall with the aim of drawing moisture towards them and evaporating it out. They work on the same principle of a wall bedded and pointed with a breathable lime mortar. However, because evaporation is concentrated at a point, there is a tendency for them to block with salts soon after installation.

Other solutions include electro osmotic systems. While these have appeared effective in certain situations, they are inconsistent in their results and therefore not generally recommended by surveyors.

Left: Many low level damp problems can be resolved by simply addressing the defects; never rely on 'miracle' cures which scar the building and are unlikely to work. In this case, both injected damp-proof courses and ceramic tubes have been tried, but problems persist.

Walls

From brick, stone and flint to wattle and daub and cob, the construction of old houses varies enormously and the materials and techniques used are almost infinite. Common to all old walls is their wonderful patina and texture which, unlike their modern equivalents, simply get better with age.

Old buildings are testimony to the skill and ingenuity of past generations of craftsmen and the diversity of materials they employed. In some areas, stones were easily won from the ground; where stone was unavailable, earth was used and, in heavily wooded regions, timber framing developed into a whole new language of construction. This use of indigenous resources gave buildings a context within their geographical setting.

Traditionally, walls were maintained and repaired in a 'like-for-like' or similar way. They were periodically altered to keep up with changing fortunes and fashions yet there was continuity in the basic palette of materials used. Unconsciously, but importantly, the principles of breathability were incorporated.

All this changed with the Industrial Revolution when the railways began carrying mass-produced materials, such as bricks, to every corner of the country. By the later nineteenth century, harder cement-based mortars and renders had crept in and the interwar period of the early twentieth century saw experimental building on a massive scale. By the 1950s, modern cavity construction had usurped the solid breathing wall.

Today, modern buildings sit side by side with the old, but the techniques and materials used in their repair are not interchangeable and are as incompatible as oil and water.

LIME

Cement as we know it was invented in 1824 for use in civil engineering projects, harbours, bridge building and the like. By the early1900s it was being gradually introduced into domestic building but traditional, solid brick walls were still commonly constructed in lime mortars. After World War II, a massive rebuilding programme required houses to be built with more prefabricated

Above: Repairing the external envelope of your home is the first step in any project. This building in Cirencester is being carefully repaired and repointed in lime mortar. In this case, the joints are brought flush in preparation for a limewash finish to reflect the local tradition.

elements and at a much faster pace. Cement-based mortars fulfilled the criteria, and traditional lime mortars disappeared almost entirely by the 1950s.

Early mortars were entirely different. In their simplest forms they were clay-based earth, dug from the ground. Such mortars are often found in rubble-stone walls where vast quantities were required to pack out the spaces between the stone. Where earth mortars were used for the core, the outer face was usually pointed with a lime-based mortar which would stand up to the rain.

One easy way of differentiating between lime and cement mortars is to take a small lump out of the wall and crumble it between your fingers. Lime will break up with relative ease as the bonds are much weaker; cement, on the other hand, will resist compressive forces and remain in a lump. Another test is to put the tip of a penknife against the mortar in the wall and lean against it. The blade will usually sink into the lime mortar but not into the cement.

All lime originates from limestone, one of the most abundant materials on the planet. There are two basic types of lime, non-hydraulic and hydraulic.

Non-hydraulic lime

Non-hydraulic lime is produced from pure limestone. It is broken down into small lumps and burnt in a kiln to drive off the carbon dioxide, converting it to calcium oxide or 'quicklime'. This is slaked with water to convert it into calcium hydroxide or 'lime putty', which is mixed with sand to produce mortars and plasters. These putty limes have the greatest breathability and flexibility and are ideal for use with soft, porous materials. Non-hydraulic limes will only cure through the absorption of carbon dioxide from the atmosphere, converting the calcium hydroxide back into calcium carbonate, a very stable and benign material. They will then last indefinitely if stored in a sealed container.

Hydraulic limes

Hydraulic limes are produced from limestones with naturally occurring impurities that contain a range of complex setting agents. They come in powder form and will start to set as soon as they come into contact with water. They should be bought fresh as they have a relatively short shelf life and must be stored in dry conditions.

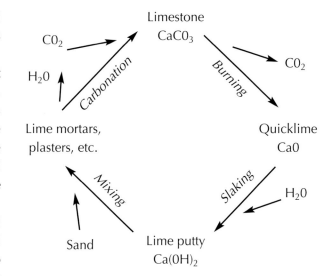

$$\text{Limestone } CaCO_3$$

Carbonation — Burning

CO_2 → · H_2O ↑ · → CO_2

Lime mortars, plasters, etc. · Quicklime CaO

Mixing — Slaking

Sand · Lime putty $Ca(OH)_2$ · ← H_2O

Above: The 'lime cycle' shows in simple terms how pure limestones are converted to non-hydraulic lime mortars, eventually absorbing carbon dioxide and returning to limestone.

They are ideal for use in a damp or exposed situation or where there is need for a higher compressive strength or a quick set. Hydraulic lime is also ideal for laying new brick or stonework.

Hydraulic limes come in a variety of strengths, for instance NHL 2, NHL 3.5 and NHL 5, depending on the proportion of clay contained in the original limestone. NHL stands for 'natural hydraulic lime' and the number reflects the compressive strength. Be cautious when selecting your lime: the higher the number, the less flexibility and breathability the mortar will have.

Hydrated or 'bagged lime'

At the risk of complicating the matter further, non-hydraulic lime also comes in a powdered form, commonly called hydrated lime. Sold by builders' merchants as an additive for cement mixes, it is used to give cement mortar more plasticity and workability. Basically, it is a powdered form of non-hydraulic lime putty. A fresh bag of hydrated lime can be soaked for a few days in a container and will thicken up to form a lime putty. However, if the hydrated lime is not fresh, or has been stored in damp conditions, the quality of the putty produced will be inconsistent and may be less durable in the longer term. It is not recommended to use hydrated lime as a substitute for slaked lime putty, since the risk of failure is not worth the small cost saving.

Below: Lime has been burnt on a large scale since the Industrial Revolution. Small field kilns were also in operation. Here, a simple, modern demonstration kiln is used to convert raw limestone into quicklime.

Bottom: After being burnt in a kiln, the large lumps of quicklime are broken up prior to slaking in a metal bath.

Choosing the right lime

With a wide variety of limes available, it is possible to find a suitable mortar or render for any situation without resorting to the use of cement. This chart gives an indication of the most appropriate choices.

HARD BRICK OR STONE	Sheltered location	NHL 2 or 3.5
	Exposed location	NHL 3.5 or 5
SOFT BRICK OR STONE	Sheltered location	Lime putty
	Exposed location	NHL 2 or 3.5
COB, STRAW BALE, TIMBER FRAME	Sheltered location	Lime putty
	Exposed location	Lime putty
OTHER SITUATIONS	High level, e.g. bedding ridge tiles, flaunching and mortar fillets, horizontal surfaces, etc.	NHL 5
	Below ground works, footings, rendering or pointing to cellars, retaining walls, etc.	NHL 3.5 or 5

Lime mortars

The correct type of lime should be selected according to the job. For laying new bricks or stones, a weak hydraulic lime is ideal. This can be mixed by hand or, for larger quantities, in a cement mixer. As hydraulic lime comes in powder form, it is mixed in a similar way to cement at a ratio of around three parts sand to one part lime. Select your sand carefully (see below) and always avoid breathing in the dust.

For general repointing to soft bricks and stones, non-hydraulic putty mortars are recommended as they are easier to apply and have greater breathability. Repointing mortars need to be relatively stiff and, if mixed in a cement mixer, tend to ball up at the back, so for small quantities it is easier to mix by hand.

Safety first

> Lime is alkaline. It can be extremely hazardous if it comes into contact with eyes.
> When working with lime, always wear goggles and have clean water and eye wash on hand.
> If you are working on a scaffold, take a flask of lukewarm water for emergency eye washing.
> Never breathe in powdered lime; it will slake on your lungs. Either use a good-quality face mask or hold your breath when opening the bag.
> While brief skin contact generally does no harm, prolonged contact will cause skin to dry out and will ultimately cause 'lime burns', typically on finger tips.
> Tight-fitting surgical gloves are ideal to protect hands.
> Always wash hands after using lime.

Above: When handling lime, it is important to be aware of the health and safety implications. Eyes are particularly vulnerable so always wear goggles if it is likely to splash and carry eye wash for emergency use.

Right: Always colour test the mortar before use, particularly if you are patch repointing. Experiment with different-coloured sharp sands and blend sands together if necessary.

Mixing mortar

To mix a lime putty mortar from scratch you will need:

> A large board.
> Mature lime putty.
> Sharp, well-graded sand, fairly dry (see box below).
> A shovel.
> Goggles and gloves.

Lime putty mortar is generally mixed at a ratio of 1:3 parts lime to sand. This ratio comes about as the air voids within a sharp, well-graded sand are approximately one-third of the volume. By adding one bucket of lime putty to three buckets of sand, you are effectively filling the voids within the sand matrix. This should therefore produce three buckets (not four) of mortar.

Sand selection

Choosing the right sand is critical to a good job. Not only will the sand dictate the colour of your mix but it will also impart a compressive strength.

When mixing cement mortar, 'soft' or 'building' sand is used. This comprises small, regular sized, rounded particles that will be 'glued' together by the cement. Using this type of sand with lime will almost certainly lead to failure of the work. Lime does not glue the sand together as cement does, but holds it in a tightly compacted matrix. In order to achieve this, sand for pointing should be 'sharp' and 'well-graded'. Sharp sand has angular edges and flat sides that interlock and resist shrinkage. Well-graded means with many different particle sizes, from dust through to a few millimetres across, filling the voids within the sand matrix.

The colour of the sand will dictate the colour of the final mortar joint and needs to be given some thought. Colour matching is particularly important if you are only patch repointing. The easiest way of selecting the right sand is to make up a series of 'mortar biscuits', allow them to dry and then snap them in half and compare them with your existing mortar.

Mixing mortar by hand is hard work. A dryish sand mixed with a stiffish lime putty may look too dry to mix, but do resist adding water. If the mortar is too sloppy, it will be impossible to control when used for repointing; it will also be prone to excessive shrinkage. To mix the mortar, chop it up and then use the back of the shovel to 'knead' it. It may help to tread it wearing a pair of rubber boots. Continue to mix until the mortar is pliable and can be moulded into a ball. If it is crumbly, it requires further mixing.

Right: 'Soft sand' is designed for use with cement. The small rounded particles are 'glued' together with the cement, forming a rigid impermeable mortar. 'Sharp, well-graded sand' is used with lime, the latter simply filling the voids between the sand particles. The closely compacted matrix gives the mortar its compressive strength while it retains flexibility and impermeability.

Top tip: Short cut to lime mortars

If sourcing the raw materials and mixing your own seems like too much hard work, consider buying your mortar ready mixed. This is a good option provided you can source a ready mix that is the right colour for your house. Your local lime supplier should be able to advise. Remember, putty mortars will last indefinitely if they are stored in sealed containers.

Mixing hydraulic limes

Hydraulic limes tend to be easier to mix than lime putties, since they come in powder form and can be used in a cement mixer. Be careful when taking the powder out of the bag (➡ Safety first, page 45) and try using an old dustbin lid to cover the mouth of the mixer. Hydraulic limes are usually mixed at a ratio of 1:2 or 1:3 parts lime to sand, depending on the strength required. Ideally it should be left in the mixer for at least 15 minutes to allow it to 'fatten up'. When using a standard cement mixer, mortar has to be mixed to a wetter consis-

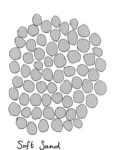

Soft Sand.

Sharp, well graded sand

tency. While this is generally suitable for plastering and laying, it is not ideal for repointing as the mortar will not be stiff enough. By tipping a wet mix on a board, covering it with plastic and leaving it overnight, it should be a firmer, 'fattier' mix the following day.

Preparing brickwork for repointing

Always leave sound lime mortar in place and simply patch repoint eroded areas where water is settling in the joints. Where repointing is required, a considerable part of the job is in the preparation. When removing old pointing, never be tempted to use mechanical tools. Angle grinders will invariably stray on to the brick face and do irreversible damage. Rake out loose, soft mortar using an old screwdriver, forming a clean square edge on which the new mortar can sit.

If you are removing hard cement pointing applied over lime mortar, a narrow plugging chisel and small lump hammer should do the job without damaging surrounding brickwork. Often modern cement has been simply smeared over the surface of the joint and is easily

Left: If the majority of the lime pointing is sound, simply patch repoint eroded joints with a matching mortar. In this case, the remaining pointing is loose and should be raked out and the wall repointed in full.

Above: Never allow your builder to use an angle grinder to remove pointing, as here, whether it is lime or cement. The dust will cloud his vision and the sharp edge of the disc will almost certainly slip on to the face of the brick or stone.

Left: For removing hard cement mortar, a plugging chisel, narrower than the joint itself, works well. Always ask your builder to demonstrate on a sample area before committing to a whole elevation.

removed. If cement pointing has been applied to a greater depth, it may be difficult to remove it without damaging soft bricks. If this is the case, you need to ask yourself if you will do more damage taking the cement pointing out than by leaving it in. This can be established by a small trial; in certain cases, cement pointing is better left in place.

Repointing

You will need:
> A bucket of putty mortar at the correct consistency.
> Water spray equipment.
> A mortar hawk (mini versions are easier to handle).
> A pointing iron or tool.
> Hessian, nails and hammer.

The pointing iron is the most important piece of equipment and it is worth finding one that is comfortable to hold and easy to use. The blade should be narrower than the actual width of joint and no longer than the 'perpend' or vertical joint between the bricks. To get the correct size, you may need to adapt an existing tool, or try making your own from a cutlery knife. A blacksmith should be able to assist quite cheaply.

Diagnosing failures in new lime pointing

If the pointing has gone very crumbly:
> The wall was not properly prepared or wetted down before the work started.
> The pointing was not kept damp after application.
> The work was carried out too late in the year and has suffered frost damage.

If the pointing has developed shrinkage cracks:
> The mortar was applied too wet.
> It was not 'pressed back' during the curing process.
> The sand was too soft and fine.

If the pointing has gone very white:
> The mortar was not finished properly during the curing process.
> The pointing was not kept damp after application.

1. Rake out a minimum of 10mm, more if required to get back to sound mortar. Clear the dust using a dry paintbrush working from the top down.

2. Wet the joint thoroughly before the work begins; if you apply new mortar to a dry joint it will not carbonate properly and will crumble and fall out. Wetting up can be done with a hose and trigger-spray or a pump-action garden spray.

Left: Repointing.

WARNING! Be sure to catch the mortar in time at stage 5. If it has started to go white, you have left it too long. Once green hard, scrape the excess mortar off the surface back to a flush finish. This will take the lime-rich layer off the surface, leaving the joint 'open textured' and able to evaporate more moisture. After stage 6, give the joint a fine mist spray and cover it with hessian to slow down drying out and encourage optimum carbonation. This is particularly important on warm or windy days.

3. Before starting, practise lifting a sliver of mortar off your hawk. If you cannot do this, you are likely to make a terrible mess of the brick face and are probably best leaving it to the professionals!

4. Apply the mortar to a clean, damp joint, working from the top down. Bring the mortar slightly proud of the brick face and avoid fiddling with it too much at this stage.

5. Wait for the mortar to go 'green hard' – between a few hours and a couple of days, depending on the volume of mortar and the temperature. Prod it with a finger to see if it makes an impression – if not, the joint is ready to be finished.

6. Finish the joint by hitting it with a stiff bristle brush. This will force the mortar to the back of the joint and close up any shrinkage cracks.

Right: Bricks may 'spall' for a variety of reasons, particularly when used with incompatible materials such as cement.

Brickwork repairs

Spalling brickwork Early bricks were fired at low temperatures and, as a result, were relatively soft. If these bricks have been subjected to excessive moisture followed by frost they tend to 'spall': the face of the brick flakes off. This is exacerbated if the bricks have been repointed with hard cement, since the moisture is forced to evaporate through the face rather than the mortar joint.

Once bricks have spalled back more than a few millimetres, they not only become unsightly but also make the penetration of damp more likely. If spalling is fairly limited, it may be feasible to repair individual brick faces. This can be done in one of two ways.

The first method is to cut out the individual bricks carefully and replace them. Assuming the mortar is soft, rake it out with hacksaw blades, old screwdrivers or

gently drill a series of holes into the joint around the brick. If you can get enough 'foothold', try an old hand-saw. Avoid the use of disc cutters: they are difficult to control and are likely to damage the surrounding bricks. If the reverse face is good, you may simply be able to turn the brick around; otherwise, choose a good matching brick (be aware that older bricks come in imperial not metric sizes). If you have a number of bricks to replace, it is possible to have a batch made specially to match by a traditional brickworks but this can be expensive. Bed the new bricks in a lime mortar which matches the colour of the existing mortar. Select your craftsman carefully: if not carried out with skill, individual brick replacement can be visually catastrophic.

The second method is to make up the face of the bricks with a tinted lime mortar. Again, if poorly executed, this can look very amateurish, but if skilfully applied it can be almost invisible to the eye. While this may not survive as long as brick replacement, in a sheltered environment it could last ten to fifteen years. Remove any loose surface material from the brick first to provide a sound key. Use a range of pigments to tint a stiff lime mortar, then apply with care. Press back the tinted mortar just before it goes off and finish the surface with a wooden tool, rather than a smooth metal trowel. Rake out around the outside to point up the brick afterwards. Bear in mind that such repairs may weather differently from the surrounding brickwork and can become more obvious over time.

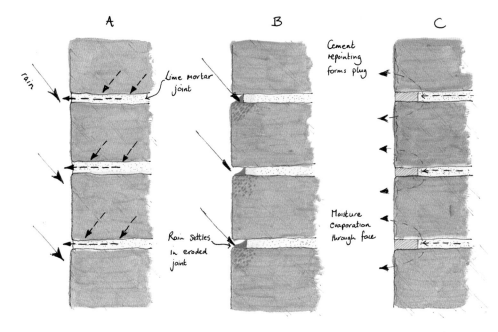

A

rain

lime mortar joint

B

Cement repointing forms plug

Rain settles in eroded joint

C

Moisture evaporation through face

A. Traditionally, walls would have been built in a soft lime mortar that was more permeable than the bricks or the stones. When walls become wet the mortar acts as a wick, drawing much of the moisture and evaporating it from the face of the joint.

B. Over time, the face of the joint erodes. The wider the joint, and the more exposed the location, the faster this will occur. It is important to repoint the wall before a ledge is formed, otherwise water will settle and cause damp penetration.

C. Walls should be repointed with a compatible mortar. Unfortunately, in recent years, hard cement has been and continues to be used. This forms a hard plug over the joint, preventing evaporation through the mortar. Instead, moisture has to evaporate through the face of the brick or stone, often causing spalling.

Above: By blending colourfast artists' pigments with lime mortar, a skilled craftsmen can make up a repair mix for the face of an old brick.

Above: Slight variations in colour tones can be even more convincing, emulating the mottled effect of the original bricks.

Above left: Individual bricks which have been bedded in lime mortar can be easily replaced or turned.

Above: Poorly executed brick replacement can be visually catastrophic. Be sure to replace old bricks with imperial sizes rather than metric sizes as happened here. If the brick is slightly smaller, the bedding joint will be wider and far more obvious.

Stitching brickwork

While the relative weakness of lime mortar will tolerate a considerable amount of movement, under severe pressures bricks will crack; for instance, localised subsidence due to a leaking drain. Once the cause of the movement has been resolved, it is sometimes necessary to replace cracked bricks. This can be done relatively easily provided you have a supply of bricks to match in size, colour and texture.

Rubbed and gauged brickwork

Rubbed and gauged brickwork refers to the high-quality work with fine joints that became popular in the eighteenth century. Typically used above window openings, but also for decorative detail on more 'polite' buildings,

Left: Rubbed and gauged brickwork is characterised by the super-fine joints between the bricks. This is achieved by 'rubbing' each individual brick to create a dead flat, square face that forms a close contact with its neighbour.

this is brickwork at its most skilful. Each brick was fashioned individually from a 'red rubber', a soft brick that could be cut to create a decorative profile or rubbed to form dead flat sides, allowing millimetre joints in between. Rubbed and gauged brickwork is definitely not a job for the average bricklayer; specialist firms can be sourced for repairs.

Tuck pointing

As the fine joints of rubbed and gauged brickwork became more fashionable, tuck pointing was developed to give the appearance of high-quality brickwork without the expense. Brickwork would be pointed up flush in mortar that matched the colour of the bricks, so the joints were almost invisible. A fine line was then indented into the mortar, just 2 or 3mm wide, and filled with a mix of lime putty and silver sand to give the impression of a very narrow joint. If you find vestiges of

Right: Tuck pointing was a cheaper alternative to rubbed and gauged work as it gave the impression of a fine joint while using ordinary bricks.

tuck pointing on your own house, you may be able to preserve a patch, or even consider reinstating it across the elevation. Again, it is not a job for the inexperienced.

STONEWORK

Stone can generally be divided into sedimentary stones such as limestones and sandstones, igneous stones such as granite, and metamorphic stones such as slates. Within these basic classifications, their colour, durability and workability varies enormously. Stones that can be split into thin slabs may be used, for instance, as roof tiles or stone flags. Stones that can be extracted from the ground in large blocks are often used as lintels. Finely grained stones, which can be worked with a chisel, are decorated or dressed into precise blocks. Historically, the characteristics of the locally available stones dictated the way in which they were used.

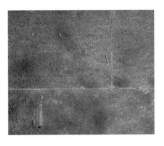

Repairing stonework

Different stones weather in different ways. Granites are tough and show little sign of erosion, whereas softer types of limestones and sandstones may erode relatively quickly, particularly in harsh environments or where exposed to industrial pollution. Cement repointing to soft stones will often cause accelerated decay. Repairing an exposed stone wall where surfaces have been partially eroded requires great skill and aesthetic judgement. Many types of stone erode gently and beautifully, imparting those subtle signs of age that you should cherish. Decaying stone is not necessarily a problem that needs putting right.

When tackling a few individual eroded stones, there are several options available:

> Leave them alone. If they have just lost their face but are still performing their function, sometimes it is better to do nothing. A little lime mortar flaunching to shed water from any ledges is advisable.

> Repair the faces with a tinted lime mortar, provided the eroded surface is not too friable. This takes skill to colour match but, in certain situations, can blend in well with the wall.

Below left: Some building stones with a high clay content, such as blue lias, are prone to expansion, resulting in surface crumbling.

Bottom left: Where stones are particularly ancient or significant, they may warrant specialist conservation techniques to preserve them in situ. In this instance, lime mortar repairs have been used to stabilise the surfaces.

Below: Stone decay is notoriously difficult to tackle. Different buildings require different approaches and materials. A hard cement has been used here in a misguided attempt to patch up early surface spalling on a house in Glasgow; it has accelerated the problem by trapping moisture.

Above: The three principal forms of stone construction.

Top: Ashlar, defined by very fine joints, often just a couple of millimetres thick. It can be achieved only with fine-grained stone capable of being dressed to a smooth finish, such as Bath stone, Portland stone and certain fine-grained sandstones.

Centre: Coursed rubble, roughly dressed stone levelled out to similar thickness and laid in courses.

Bottom: Random rubble, stone taken directly from the ground laid in a wall in random sizes.

> Remove the whole stone or chisel back the eroded section and piece in a new face. The replacement piece should match the original stone as closely as possible, otherwise complex chemical reactions between the two stones may be triggered. Always try to reinstate the original mortar joints, rather than replacing two separate stones with a single patch.

The final choice of repair solution will largely depend on the individual building. For instance, when repairing a fine Georgian ashlar facade it is important to conserve the simplicity of the lines and the overall architectural intention; this may necessitate replacement of eroded stone with new stone to match. On the other hand, with a 'crumbly' medieval building, keeping the maximum historic fabric should be paramount and this may be best achieved with tile or mortar repairs. You may need to adopt a different approach to stones that have a structural function from ones that are decorative or simply ordinary walling.

The location of damaged stonework may also influence the choice of repair. For example, an eroded stone face at low level may be simply monitored and left alone. Damaged stonework to a parapet, where it is taking a beating from the weather, may be best replaced during reproofing works to minimise expensive scaffolding.

Cleaning stonework

The subject of cleaning stonework has been much debated in recent years. It is often suggested that a certain level of dirt to a building's facade can visually enhance its appearance. Certainly, there have been many cleaning disasters when inappropriate chemicals, water washing or sand blasting have caused accelerated surface decay. Before embarking on any stone cleaning programme, ask yourself if it is really necessary. If in doubt, do not clean.

Where soot and dirt have built up on the surface and may be causing damage, research and small-scale testing should be carried out before any large-scale cleaning operation is begun. Bear in mind that limestone and sandstone have very dissimilar chemistry and require different cleaning methods. The dirt build-up on limestone is usually water-soluble: gentle washing techniques, using the minimum amount of water, will usually achieve a level of success. Sandstone buildings usually require chemical cleaning agents and these are

Left: When replacing whole stones it is generally best to reinstate them to their original profile rather than to match their eroded neighbours. This will maintain the line of the wall.

Left: 'Tile' repairs are a good option in specific situations. They allow the minimum amount of eroded stone to be taken out and pieces of handmade clay tiles or stone slips to be 'layered' with lime mortar to fill the space.

Left: Larger areas of stone erosion are more problematic and, before tackling repairs, it is worth addressing the underlying cause of the problem. Rather than replacing stones to an extensively damaged face, it may be an option to render the elevation. This will act as a 'sacrificial' coat and arrest further erosion to the stone itself.

Right: You should think hard about whether your building does need cleaning. If it does, stone cleaning should never be embarked upon without extensive trials. Here a chemical has been used to remove dirt from sandstone. It is critical to follow neutralising instructions to the letter as chemicals can continue to attack the face of the stone for many weeks after the initial trials.

Opposite, far right: Flint was commonly used for walling right across the 'flint belt' in East Anglia and the south-east of England where it was easily won from the ground. In this example in West Sussex, it has been knapped to form the window surrounds, contrasting with the grey nodules employed for the bulk of the wall.

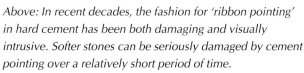

Above: In recent decades, the fashion for 'ribbon pointing' in hard cement has been both damaging and visually intrusive. Softer stones can be seriously damaged by cement pointing over a relatively short period of time.

specific to the particular type of stone you are dealing with. Your conservation officer will usually be able to offer specific advice on your local building stones.

Repointing stonework

Repointing ashlar work is extremely skilful and should be left to professionals. Rubble stonework, on the other hand, is relatively easy to repoint for the dextrous amateur. Traditional pointing was usually brought flush, sometimes leaving only the highest peaks of the stones exposed. Bear in mind that much rubble work was originally finished either with limewash, roughcast or smooth render. Rarely was it left as exposed stone unless it was decorated with 'gallets'.

If you are intending to render your rubble stone, the exercise of repointing is particularly easy: it does not matter how it looks, provided it is technically sound. However, if your stonework is to be left exposed, great

Above: 'Gallets' or 'pinnings' were used to pack out wide joints in rubble stonework but, in certain areas, they were also used to decorative effect. When repointing such a wall it is important to reinstate these vernacular details.

Left: While repointing stonework is largely the same as brickwork, there are a couple of differences. After cleaning out the joint and wetting up, proceed thus:

1. Push the mortar to the back of the joint, bringing it slightly proud of the face; a plasterer's small tool is the ideal implement.

2. For larger voids, say greater than 15mm cubed, pack the joint with small stones, known as 'gallets' or 'pinnings'. These will reduce the mortar required, and hence the resultant shrinkage.

3. Once green hard, scrape off excess mortar and take it back to a flush finish. Beat the joint with a stiff bristle brush.

4. The finished joint should have an open texture for maximum breathability and be free from cracks. Remember to protect the joint from drying out too quickly by covering it in damp hessian.

care should be taken to select an appropriate mortar colour and leave a neat surface finish.

The pointing mortar for rubble stone may use a coarser sand than that for brickwork. As a general rule, look at the average joint width. For example, if this is 15mm, divide by three to give 5mm, then choose a well-graded sand with a maximum particle size of 5mm. By increasing the particle size you will reduce the shrinkage in the mortar.

Flintwork

While the general rules of masonry repair apply to flint, there are a few peculiarities that need to be taken into account. Flint can be used as whole nodules or, for better work, 'knapped', meaning split to expose its shiny inner face. For better-quality walls, 'flushwork' was used in which a flint nodule was knapped on five sides to create a square block with thin joints.

Knapping, in which a blunt instrument is used to chip the flint into the desired shape, requires great skill. Once

Above: The rounded shape of the flint nodules are difficult to build with as there are no flat edges. Sometimes flint chippings are used as 'gallets' to wedge the nodules in place and reduce the quantity of mortar while also providing a decorative effect.

Above right: The finest flint walling is called 'flushwork', where nodules are squared and knapped to dress them to a specific shape and combined with stone.

formed, the flints are virtually indestructible and not subject to any of the decay mechanisms suffered by other stones. The weakness of a flint wall is due to the shape of the individual nodules: imagine building a wall out of tennis balls with no flat sides on which to bed them. Consequently, flint is prone to whole sheets of facework becoming detached from the core. This is exacerbated if the flint is pointed with cement: it prevents drainage of the wall and hydrostatic pressure can build up in the core, eventually causing the outer face to blister off.

Where a whole section of facework has come away, it is a painstaking job to rebuild, tying the new work back to the core of the wall at regular intervals. Where voids have developed behind, causing the face to bulge, it may be possible to inject a lime-based grout to stabilise the wall. These techniques are difficult and complex and should be carried out by an experienced craftsman.

Houses built largely of flint can cause difficulties when it comes to internal fittings such as cupboards and pipes, since it is impossible to drill into flint. Small wooden plugs or embedded timbers were often incorporated during construction in order to facilitate fixings.

EARTH

Earth construction was used extensively due to its cheapness and availability. The techniques employed vary enormously across the country but they fall into some basic categories.

Wattle and daub

Wattle and daub was the technique for filling the spaces of a timber-framed building. Vernacular techniques varied enormously, but this was commonly achieved using a woven panel of sticks (wattlework) on to which a sticky mud mixture was pressed (daub). Such ancient methods continued in rural areas up to the nineteenth

century: the materials were free and little skill was required. Those who could afford to tended to replace wattle and daub panels with the more fashionable brick; as a result, few original panels remain.

If you are removing a cement render from an ancient timber frame, you may expose an original wattle and daub panel. Trapped moisture behind the hard render may have caused some deterioration. Always remove the cement render gently – this is one of the few occasions when a small disc cutter may be useful to form a grid across the hard surface, allowing each bit to be gently levered off.

Once exposed, assess the condition of the daub; it may need simple re-rendering with lime plaster. If the daub is friable and loose, gently take away the affected area, collecting the old daub to be reconstituted in the new mix.

The condition of the 'withies' (horizontal woven twigs) and 'staves' (vertical sticks) must also be assessed

where they are exposed. Often ancient wattlework suffers woodworm and loses its structural integrity. If this is the case, gently pick out the affected withies and weave new hazel rods or riven laths in their place. Where a panel has completely disintegrated and is beyond repair, or has to be dismantled during works to the timber frame, a new panel can be formed from scratch. Again, always save the old daub for re-use.

Ready-made daub can be purchased from specialist suppliers but it is strongly recommended that you mix your own. It is simply a mixture of sticky, clay-based earth, straw and water. The original mud used will almost certainly have been dug from earth around your house: a subsoil with a good clay content, rather than topsoil which has no structural cohesion.

Once you have sourced new earth, lay it on a board, remove large stones and break up the lumps – a long-handled sledge hammer is ideal for this. Include any salvaged daub, sprinkle on loose straw and mix together,

Above: Some timber-framed buildings, such as this one in Surrey, have been completely 'reinvented' in the last hundred years, with the fashion for painting the timbers black and the wattle and daub panels white.

Far left: Cement render can do great damage to a wattle and daub panel, trapping moisture behind it. Removal of the cement should be carried out with care to save as much historic fabric as possible.

Left: Wormy or rotten withies can be replaced with new hazel rods or riven oak laths.

Far left: New wattlework panels can be easily fitted.

Left: The key to a successful daub is a stiff consistency. If it is too wet, it will slump and be impossible to form around the wattlework. Instead, the daub should be the consistency of Plasticine.

Far left: When applying the daub to the wattle panel, push the mix through the sticks so that it wraps around each one.

Left: Build up the daub in horizontal layers and try to minimise air voids by forcing it into every crevice and through to the other side. Once the face is complete, and before the daub starts to dry out, build up the reverse face and integrate it with the mix that has squashed through the wattlework. Better still, recruit another person to work from the other side of the panel so you can build up the daub on both faces at the same time.

fairly dry. Finally, add water, a little at a time, and continue to mix until the daub is sticky and pliable. Treading the mix is a good way to achieve this and cattle were often used in the past, hence the cow dung that is sometimes found in daub mixes! However, dung is not a necessary ingredient of daub.

The daub takes between a few days and a few weeks to dry, depending on the time of year and the thickness of the panel. Once dry, it needs to be finished with non-hydraulic lime plaster and limewash. In anticipation of this, set the face of the daub back by 10mm from the plane of the timber frame to allow the plaster to be finished flush. Using a wooden stick, scratch the surface of the daub in a criss-cross pattern to provide a key for the plaster; this is best done while the daub is still sticky. Once fully dry, apply one or two coats of plaster depending on the flatness of finish required.

Cob

This is the common word used to describe mass earth walls, using clay-based subsoil mixed with straw and water to a gooey consistency and built up about a foot at a time. The result is a monolithic structure, often 600mm or more thick. Cob has often been unwittingly rendered in cement and may appear to be a rubble stone construction, deceiving both surveyors and home-owners.

Cob houses tend to have wide overhanging eaves to minimise contact between the walls and rain. Cob is usually set on a masonry plinth, which is where the wall is most vulnerable to damp. These design features are zjknown as 'a good hat and a good pair of boots'.

Earth used in this way can last many centuries, provided it is maintained and protected from excessive amounts of damp. Water is the principal enemy of earthen walls. Unlike brick or stone which retain their compressive strength in damp situations, earth will soften and lose its structural stability.

Common causes of failure in cob walls are:
> Leaking roof or failing gutter, causing concentrated trickles of water to run down the surface or into the wall head. Over time, this will soften the earth and it will lose its structural stability.
> Cement render. This is incompatible on cob, and particularly bad news if it is cracked, since water will become trapped behind it. As the moisture levels rise, the load-bearing capacity of the earth wall will diminish.

Below: Earth structures can last for centuries provided they are kept dry. Here, a hole to the thatch has allowed water to wash away the mud wall directly beneath and undermine the structure. In addition, cattle have rubbed against the corner.

Left: Wide overhanging eaves and a masonry plinth are essential features of a long-lasting earth building.

Repairs to cob walls

Once cement render is removed, it is likely that a cob wall will require some degree of repair. Often the walls will be damaged either at the top or the bottom where they have most contact with water. This often results in dips and hollows in the surface, but these cannot be dubbed out by slapping on a new cob mix of earth and straw as it will not adhere. Cob is effectively a masonry construction; unlike the infill panels of wattle and daub, cob is acting in compression to carry the load of the walls and roof. With this in mind, any repairs should be made up in horizontal layers to carry the forces acting from above. One of the simplest methods of achieving this is to make or buy cob blocks.

Once the blocks have dried, cut away the damaged section of wall ready to receive them. Try to cut back to square edges to form a snug fit with the new blocks. Bed the blocks in an earth mortar made from the same subsoil, or salvage the original cob mix that you have cut away to form the hole. Sieve the earth to remove larger stones and mix with a little water to form a good sticky mortar ideal for bedding the blocks.

> High external ground level, where damp ground rises above the masonry plinth and comes into contact with the earth wall.
> Rat runs. Cob walls are particularly vulnerable to rodents burrowing through them. Providing the rat runs are redundant the odd one will do no harm, but a large network of runs may undermine structural stability.

Above: Lack of maintenance of the gutter and roof, combined with a hard cement render, have all contributed to the decay of this cob cottage in Ireland. The roof would probably have been originally thatched, providing a good overhang to throw the rain clear of the walls.

Below: Pre-formed earth or cob blocks, bedded in an earth slurry, are used to make up a damaged corner to a mud building in Leicestershire.

Below: Once dry, the corner is finished by cutting away the sharp edges before applying an earth and lime render.

Top tip: Approach with care

If you are tackling a cob wall with a cement-rendered finish, be cautious before removing it, particularly if the building is in a derelict condition. There have been instances where the cob has washed away behind the render, and the cement is all that is holding the building up! To investigate its condition, use an angle grinder to cut a square out of the render and gently lever it off. Never attempt to lever off large sheets of cement render in one go since they could be performing a structural function.

Other earth traditions

As well as the more common wattle and daub and cob, there were many other vernacular traditions using earth as a basic building material. Some of the more interesting included:

> 'Clay lump', a technique of mass earth building which tends to be found in Suffolk and Norfolk. Developed in the eighteenth century, it employed preformed blocks of sun-baked earth bedded in earth mortar.

> 'Wytchert', literally translated as 'white earth', using the chalky clays of Buckinghamshire in a similar technique to cob.

> 'Mud and stud', developed in Lincolnshire, combining a flimsy timber frame encased in earth, rather like a combination of wattle and daub and cob.

> Numerous other variations on cob, for instance 'clom' in West Wales, 'mud' in the Midlands and 'clay dabbins' in Cumbria.

Each of these vernacular traditions should be carefully understood before attempting repairs. Commonsense is the watchword, putting back like-for-like materials and calling upon local specialists.

CLADDING SYSTEMS

In an exposed location, wind-driven rain can present a problem with traditional wall constructions. Especially in the case of timber-framed houses with wattle and daub infill, water can penetrate the junction between the panel and the frame or become trapped on the top of the rail causing decay. Even on a dry day, such buildings are prone to draughts and heat loss.

Due partly to these practical issues but also to fashion, many buildings were clad in some way, either at the time they were built, or some time later. In its simplest form, this may have involved a coating of lime render but clay tiles, slates, weatherboarding and mathematical tiles have all been used.

Tile hanging

Clay tiles or slates were used to clad external walls, usually fixed to timber battens. The most common problems with tile hanging occur when the battens rot or the nails holding the tiles rust; repairs are much the same as those to roofs.

Top: Mud and stud cottage in Lincolnshire prior to repair.

Above: The same building after careful conservation work and traditional repair.

Weatherboarding

Weatherboarding was a common cladding particularly to timber-framed buildings.

The simplest form was waney-edge oak or elm. These boards, with their bark left on and natural undulations, were a traditional finish for farm buildings and became fashionable for domestic buildings in the nineteenth century. More commonly, painted regular-width soft-wood boards were used. Although cheap forms of sawn 'shiplap' boarding are stocked by timber merchants, these are unlikely to match the original, so specially milled boards may have to be ordered for repairs.

Mathematical tiles

These were tiles designed to look like brickwork, applied to give a more fashionable facade to buildings such as timber-framed structures. They were set out on battens to clad the elevations and were extremely convincing – in fact, they continue to fool many a surveyor! The giveaway is on the corner where they often meet a rendered side elevation with an awkward junction. It may be possible to get standard sizes for repair but it is more likely that 'specials' would have to be made by a brickyard.

Above: Tile hanging was often an afterthought and an attempt to keep out wind-driven rain. However, in certain areas, tile hanging using decorative shapes became a fashionable finish.

Right: Mathematical tiles are nailed in place in the same way as hanging tiles, but are set out to resemble brick courses. The joints are then pointed in lime mortar.

Above: Various attempts have been made to clad the rubble stone wall of this building which stands in an exposed location near Truro, Cornwall.

Right: Weatherboarding is mainly found in the south-east; this example is from an extension to a pair of early nineteenth-century brick cottages in Highgate, London. Eighteenth-century examples often have broad boards, while later ones sometimes have a beaded edge.

Structural movement

Opposite: Temporary shoring will buy you time while you work out exactly what is required. This bulging wall appeared to be in a perilous state but could not be repaired until a structural engineer made a full assessment. Much of the movement was found to be historic and very little rebuilding was required.

Cracks, bulges and out-of-plumb walls can look rather alarming but do not panic! Traditional buildings were built with materials that could accommodate some shifting of the structure. The key is to differentiate between benign historic movement and ongoing structural failure before rushing in.

Old buildings rarely come in right-angled packages, but will invariably have suffered some sort of structural movement during their lifetime. This may be due to shallow foundations, the failure of a structural element, or even poorly considered alterations.

Whereas modern buildings are constructed on deep and solid concrete foundations, many old buildings were put directly on the earth, often just a few inches below ground level. A strip of topsoil would have been scraped away to reveal the more solid subsoil, on to which bricks or stones would have been laid, bedded in lime mortar, to form the footing to the wall. Despite these seemingly inadequate footings, they have stood the test of time and, in most cases, are perfectly sound.

Poor maintenance is often the catalyst to structural failure. An ongoing drip from a missing slate will, over time, rot a key timber element, while a leaking drain may result in subsidence. Structural work to buildings also causes many problems because of inadequate propping during the works, redistribution of loading or the imposition of rigid structures upon flexible buildings. Consequently, great care needs to be taken to think through any alterations or repairs; if in doubt, seek

advice from a structural engineer specialising in old buildings.

Footings and settlement

Unlike the rigid cement-based structures of today, traditional buildings were made out of soft, flexible materials. In the early years after their completion, it was common for them to 'settle' as the ground beneath them was compressed. The structure would have moved and cracked to varying degrees, depending on the load-bearing capacity of the earth and the weight of the building. Differential settlement resulted when one part of the building was substantially heavier than the rest. For instance, it is often noticeable in churches that the tower or spire settled to a greater degree than the nave, because of its extra height and therefore weight. As the

Above: Neglected, penetrated by water and suffering from severe decay, this timber-framed building has numerous structural failings and is in a state of impending collapse, but still has the potential to be saved.

The importance of lime

The relative weakness of a lime mortar is its greatest advantage. As old buildings are made on shallow foundations, they frequently move over time. Weak lime mortar will allow this movement to occur across a large area; and through the mortar joint rather than through the bricks or stones. Cement mortars will resist any movement as long as they possibly can, until the forces have built up, at which point a crack will appear at the weakest point, usually through the bricks themselves.

Above: Settlement can be dramatically obvious but is not necessarily a cause for concern if it occurred many years ago.

Below: Subsidence is often historic and not ongoing. In this case, a leaking down pipe caused the earth to soften and the masonry above to subside. The downpipe has since been repaired but the house retains evidence of past movement.

lime mortar in the core of the walls remained soft for a considerable time, this movement stood a good chance of being tolerated within the overall structure.

Any cracks or movement resulting from initial settlement are therefore historic and not generally a cause for concern.

Subsidence and heave

The terms 'subsidence' and 'settlement' are often used interchangeably. Strictly speaking, subsidence refers to the earth beneath a footing giving way, due to external conditions, long after the house has 'settled'. There are various reasons why a building might 'subside'. For instance, a leaking drain, near to or passing under a

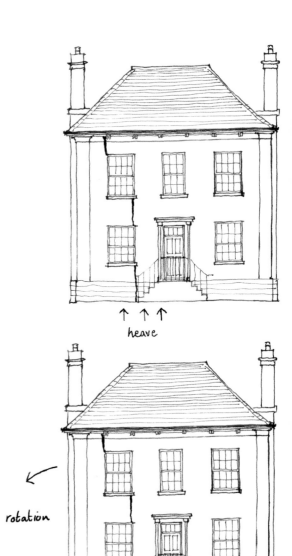

heave

rotation

settlement

Opposite: Cracks can be easily misinterpreted and, when they are, unnecessary and expensive work will often follow. Experts will look at the shape of a crack and try to establish which part has moved and which part has remained static.

Top: A tapered crack, wider at the top than the bottom, may indicate upward thrust due to heave.

Centre: But it could also indicate that part of the building is 'rotating', in this case maybe because of differential settlement from the weight of the masonry chimney stack.

Bottom: A diagonal crack is often symptomatic of localised subsidence. This could be due to a broken drain softening the ground beneath the corner.

Above right: Buildings and trees in close proximity are not a good mix. Remarkably, in this case, there are no outward signs of damage.

Below right: A tapered crack which is wider at the top than at the bottom is often indicative of 'heave', in this instance caused by tree roots close to the base of the wall.

Far right: Buildings with shallow foundations on shrinkable clay soils are often vulnerable to seasonal movement. The crack to this archway will open and close throughout the year.

building, or an underground spring, washing away or softening the soil, may result in part of the structure dropping. In some areas, old mine workings can cause subsidence, long after the mine has been decommissioned, so be sure to take this into account if such workings are identified in a 'search' during the purchase of a property.

Subsidence tends to affect a localised part of a building, following a change in the load-bearing capacity of the soil directly beneath. Tree roots, droughts and heavy frosts may all contribute to part of a building subsiding and separating itself from the rest of the structure. Such damage can, to a certain extent, be diagnosed by analysing the resulting cracks.

Heave is the opposite of subsidence. Whereas subsidence is the result of the earth giving way beneath the building, heave is caused by swelling of the earth, causing an upward thrust.

Soil types and seasonal movement

The type of ground upon which your building sits may cause it to shift slightly throughout the year. If your house is built on shrinkable clays and has shallow foundations, it is likely that it will be subject to seasonal movement in extreme weather conditions. In heavy frosts the earth may 'heave' and, during droughts, the earth may shrink and crack, leading potentially to subsidence. While this sounds alarming, a building that has stood for hundreds of years on shrinkable clays will have been exposed to such movement many times before. By monitoring a crack, you can establish whether it opens and closes with the seasons and is therefore directly attributable to seasonal movement. Provided it gets no worse year on year, it may require no further action. When analysing a crack, it is useful to know what type of soil your building sits on.

Trees and ivy

Shrubs and trees can be damaging if growing too close to the base of a wall. If the roots pass under the building, they may draw moisture out of the soil and cause it to dry and shrink, particularly with clay soils. If the soil under the footing shrinks, the section of wall is vulnerable to subsidence; this can usually be identified by a corresponding tapered crack.

Trees to be particularly wary of include poplar, oak, elm, willow and ash, although any tree adjacent to a house should be monitored. The solution is not simply to cut down the tree – this can, in turn, disturb the moisture equilibrium of the soil. If a tree that was taking water from the earth ceases to do so, the ground may become waterlogged causing heave to occur over several years. This is particularly likely if the tree predates the building. Crown and root pruning are a means of managing any risk, since these reduce the moisture taken from the soil yet leave adequate live vegetation to continue to sap up any excess. A tree can also be an indirect cause of subsidence when its roots damage drains, in turn causing

Above: Bay windows are notorious for movement problems. In this instance, the bay was added at a later stage on extremely limited footings.

Above right: Balancing nature with the wellbeing of a house is vital. Prompt action should always be taken to keep foliage under control in order to prevent damage to walls and blockages to downpipes and drains.

no damage to masonry may block gutters and hoppers and can lift roof tiles if not controlled. Foliage may also stop walls from drying out, notably on a northern elevation where air circulation on an exposed site could be critical to avoid dampness.

Assessing the condition

While structural analysis is never a job for the amateur, there are pointers that a homeowner can look out for:

> Windows and doors that suddenly start to stick or bind. Make sure this is not simply swelling of the timber in the damp winter months.
> New cracks in walls. This can be associated with drying shrinkage, particularly after a central heating system has been installed.
> Tapered cracks running diagonally from the corner of doors or windows. An opening in a wall is a weak point, and any movement is likely to emanate from these areas.
> Floors that slope. This is often due to historic settlement of the external wall but could be indicative of ongoing subsidence.
> Cracks to render or plaster at the top of a window. These may suggest rot present in the bearing end of a timber lintel.
> Look for cracks at the junction between a bay window and a main wall: bay windows are often poorly tied to the main structure.

Monitoring movement

By monitoring cracks over time, it is possible to establish whether they are on the move and whether professional

leaks that soften the soil or wash it away. A drain survey will ascertain whether this is the problem.

Old buildings are often associated with ivy-clad walls and roses around the door, but vegetation can be problematic when not carefully controlled. Ivy is the worst culprit, especially when pointing is defective. Ivy will take root in crevices and work its way into the centre of the wall, particularly on rubble stone which may have an earth core. Over time, ivy grows and expands, and will eventually blow apart great sections of masonry and destabilise walls. Do not be tempted to rip live ivy off a wall once it has established a firm hold – this may cause even greater damage. Instead, it is best to cut it off at its root, poison the stump, and allow the plant to die back gradually.

Any plant growing up the side of a building may cause problems if left unchecked. Buddleia is particularly pernicious and can take root in the most unlikely places with little encouragement. Even climbers that do

Top tip: Beware of recent alterations

If you are buying a house that has been radically altered in recent years, make sure that the work was properly thought through.

> Has a chimney breast been removed or a new door opening created without adequate support to the masonry above?
> Have internal walls been taken down to create an open-plan space?
> Do not assume that a stud wall is never load-bearing.

Signs of historic movement

Left: This structural movement is typical of a Georgian facade with tall sash windows sited one above another. The openings act as a weak point between the columns of masonry each side, and any slight movement will occur along this line.

Buildings often show signs of having moved in the past. Although not necessarily a cause for concern, these are useful indicators and worth regular monitoring. Examples include:

> Doors that have been trimmed to fit a tapered opening. If the gap around the door remains constant, no further movement has occurred.

> Skirting boards that have been scribed to accommodate a dipping floor. Look out for any future gap between the floorboards and the skirting.

> Cracks that have been repointed. If they have not opened up again since, movement has ceased.

> Spreader plates and tie rods. These were usually fitted retrospectively to provide lateral restraint to a bulging wall. While they may have resolved the problem, it is worth keeping an eye on this vulnerable area.

Right: An elegantly designed spreader plate has been fitted to retain the gable of this house. Its presence points to a past problem; monitoring is certainly worthwhile to spot any ongoing movement.

advice is necessary. The simplest way to ascertain whether a hairline crack is 'live' is to put a sharp pencil mark at the point where it ends. Date the mark, with your name, and repeat the process on a regular basis if the crack continues to grow.

When monitoring wider cracks, it is useful to fill them and record the date; if the crack opens up after filling it is clear that it is still 'live'. Externally, cracks should be filled with lime mortar to prevent water ingress; ensure this is properly applied to negate shrinkage of the mortar which could be confused with structural movement. Internally, proprietary filler will suffice.

Underpinning for subsidence

If you suspect that your home has a subsidence problem, you will need to inform your insurance company. They will appoint an assessor to take the claim forward and a structural engineer may be assigned to investigate the cause further. This sometimes involves digging trial trenches and root testing; in the worst case, underpinning may be recommended. This is a highly invasive route and one that should not be pursued unless absolutely necessary.

Where a building is prone to slight seasonal movement, imposing rigidity on one section by underpinning could lead to further problems. Whereas previously the whole building would have shifted slightly, the underpinned section could part company with the rest of the structure if it is held rigidly in position.

Underpinning may be too heavy-handed a way of dealing with minor movement at the base of an old wall. For instance, it is common for a localised area of ground to be disrupted, perhaps through a collapsed drain, and the masonry directly above may drop. In such instances, a more gentle approach may simply be to 'underbuild' the section of wall using bricks or stones bedded in hydraulic lime mortar, just a few courses down, to re-establish contact with firm ground and put the masonry back into compression.

Bulging and leaning walls

The walls of an old house will rarely be plumb or even flat. 'Defects' such as bulging and leaning walls are often the very thing that give our homes character. It is important to establish whether such characteristics are benign or active; if you have any concerns, consult a structural engineer.

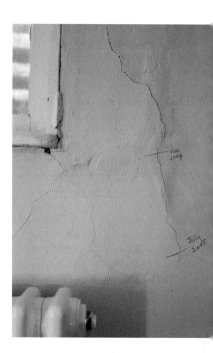

Above: Monitoring signs of movement within a house is the first step in determining the nature of a problem. By regularly marking and dating the end of a crack, it is possible to establish whether it is 'live' and the rate at which it is growing.

Above: The inner and outer 'skins' of a solid brick wall should be held together by the bonding pattern of the brickwork.

Above, second from left: Flemish bond brickwork utilises alternate 'headers' and 'stretchers' within the same course to tie the inner and outer leaves.

Above, third from left: English garden wall bond brickwork consists of three courses of stretchers and one of headers, making a distinctive pattern.

Above far right: Stretcher bond brickwork indicates a single-leaf wall or a more modern cavity wall.

Right: When the masonry of rubble stone walls is poorly tied together, they are susceptible to bulging, particularly if earth mortars in the 'core' become damp and swell.

If a wall is bulging on the outside, check whether there is a corresponding 'hollow' inside the house. In other words, has the wall shifted as a whole or have the inner and outer leaves parted company? Solid brick walls were usually constructed with a bonding pattern that tied the inner and outer 'skins' securely together. However, this did not always happen and the two can be unattached.

The Georgians, in particular, were guilty of this type of building practice. A typical terrace would have had a carcass constructed in brick, often put up in a hurry, incorporating 'bonding timbers' for added stiffness to the flimsy walls. The brick or ashlar front was frequently built by a different, highly skilled, brickmason to give the appearance of quality, but was not tied in to the carcass. In such instances, the two skins can separate and display signs of bulging to one of the faces. This is particularly problematic next to busy roads where traffic vibration over time can cause loose fragments between the skins to drop down and 'ratchet' them apart.

An additional problem with such houses is that the out-of-sequence construction often resulted in 'spine walls' (those running front to back) not being tied into the front. As a result, 'bellying' of the front wall due to lack of restraint is a common problem.

Rubble stone walls are also prone to bulging if the masonry was poorly tied in to start with. This may be triggered by dampness entering the wall and swelling the 'earth core' in the centre. Alternatively, highly concentrated loads, for example at the end of a principal beam, may cause localised bulging to the inner skin only.

Flint walls have a tendency to bulge as the rounded shape of the individual stones made it difficult to form a strong bond. A bulge in a flint wall should always be investigated.

Occasionally where walls have bulged, the joists become separated and lose their bearing. This can be relatively easily resolved by using bespoke 'joist extenders'. A limited number of boards to the floor above will require careful lifting and a narrow strip of ceiling will need to be removed. The joist extenders can then be slipped up through the gap and rotated to fit.

Arches and lintels

Brick and stone arches are complex structures. They rely on a sideways compressive force in order to retain their shape. Any general movement to a wall may allow an arch to relax out of compression so it sags or drops. It is often possible for a skilled craftsman to reset a sagging arch with minimal interference. This may be achieved by using wedges or replacing a failed 'voussoir' to put it back into compression. Alternatively, an arch may simply be supported using purpose-made steel supports.

Left: Joist extenders in the process of being fitted. Note the rebate cut into the top surface of the joist to allow the joist extender to sit 'flush' prior to refixing the old floorboards.

Right: Sometimes a simple solution is best. Rather than rebuilding a section of this wall, the arch has been repaired with a purpose-made and fully reversible stainless steel support.

Below: As the front wall of this building 'bellied' or bulged outwards, the joists to the first floor no longer met the brickwork on which they were originally supported. (A) It would have been possible to dismantle the 300-year-old wall and rebuild it 'plumb'. Alternatively, the joists could have been replaced with longer lengths to meet the wall, but this would have involved removing the historic plaster ceiling and the elm boards above. Both solutions would have been extremely invasive, involving extensive loss of fabric. The simplest solution was to design and fit purpose-made 'joist extenders' (B). These could be fitted in situ, slipped around the gap between the end of the joists and the wall (C) and rotated into position (D), all with minimum disturbance to the historic fabric. Once built into the masonry, they provide lateral restraint to resist further bulging (E).

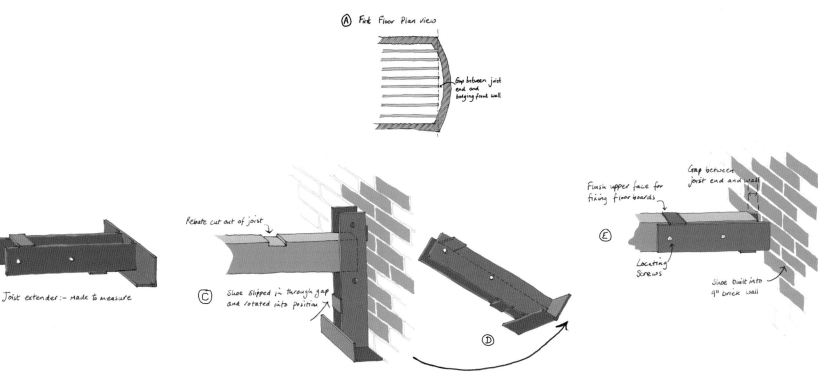

(A) First Floor Plan view

Gap between joist end and bulging front wall

Joist extender:- made to measure

Rebate cut out of joist

(C) Shoe slipped in through gap and rotated into position

(D)

Flush upper face for fixing floor boards

Gap between joist end and wall

(E)

Locating Screws

Shoe built into 9" brick wall

Most lintels in domestic buildings were formed of timber, generally oak. They were almost always concealed with plaster or render. Oak is a very strong and durable material, capable of lasting for centuries. Where failure does occur, it is usually due to a prolonged period of water ingress causing rot or beetle decay, often to the bearing ends. This is indicated by cracking to the plaster or render, as the timber compresses under load.

Stone lintels are common in certain parts of the country. It is not unusual to find cracks through the centre of such lintels where the building has shifted slightly and redistributed its loading. Such cracks are not necessarily a cause for concern, as the lintel may have locked itself into position and ceased to move. None the less, such cracks should be monitored.

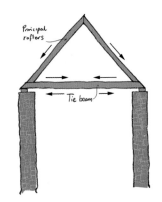
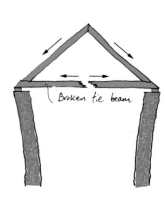

Above: Think of a roof truss as a triangle. While it is triangulated, it is very strong and can withstand *considerable forces. But if the tie beam fails or is cut through, for instance to form a door, the roof may 'spread'.*

Roofs

Roofs are particularly prone to structural movement. Not only are they subjected to changing loads, they are also vulnerable to rot and joint failure. A roof that dips along its ridge line is not necessarily in distress; roof structures can often be repaired and strengthened in situ while retaining the distortion that gives them their essential character.

Repairs can be fairly simple; in this case, one made to a cracked principal rafter in the nineteenth century uses a steel plate bolted in place.

Roof spread and racking

Some roofs were built without tie beams where attic spaces were designed to be habitable rooms. However, where tie beams were incorporated they play a crucial role in the structure by triangulating the principal rafters

and resisting the loading of the roof. If a tie beam fails, or is cut through (often to create a doorway or extra head-room in an attic), the forces on the structure are re-distributed, leading to 'roof spread'.

Racking is another common problem in roofs that have not had adequate diagonal bracing. Imagine your trussed rafters as a series of dominoes: any sideways force on one truss could push each truss out of its vertical plane. It is often possible to strengthen a racking roof in situ, by simply inserting retrospective braces. This may be achieved without straightening the trusses. A structural engineer should always be consulted.

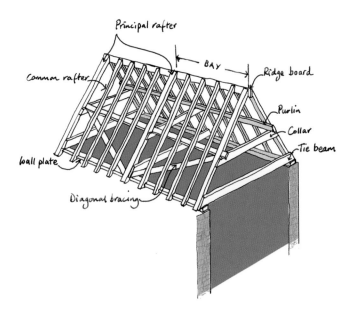

Left: Early roofs tended to be massively over-engineered, with timber sections that far surpassed their loading requirement. These were gradually refined, and the same basic roof construction has remained relatively unchanged to the present day. Roofs are divided into 'bays' by the 'principal rafters'. These are triangulated with a 'tie beam' at the bottom to form a 'truss'. The principal rafters *support the 'purlins', which in turn support the 'common rafters' at mid-span. A 'collar' is often incorporated within the truss arrangement to relieve stress on the principal rafter. A 'ridge plate' ties the common rafters together at the apex, and 'diagonal bracing' resists the sideways forces on the structure. The whole arrangement is fixed to the top of the walls by means of a 'wall plate'.*

Right: To address roof 'spread', these rafters have been restrained with tie bars while their feet have been braced with purpose-made metal brackets bolted down into the top of the wall.

Right: Diagonal bracing is a critical part of a roof structure. Where it is missing, the whole roof is vulnerable to 'racking'. A racking roof may also destabilise a gable end wall.

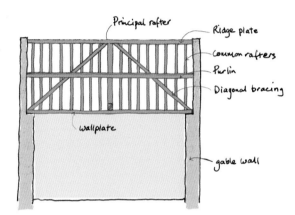

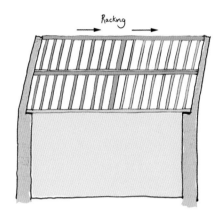

Right: An extreme example of a racking roof in Leominster. Although it looks alarming, the forces have been resolved by internal strengthening, and the roof is now held securely in this position.

Cracks: summary

> Don't panic! It may well be nothing to worry about.
> Inform your insurance company.
> Monitor the crack and record any further movement.
> Check whether the crack opens and closes with the seasons.
> Anything more than a hairline crack should generally be investigated.
> External cracks should be pointed with lime mortar to prevent moisture ingress.
> If you have any doubts, consult a structural engineer with experience in old buildings.
> If you're unhappy with your structural engineer's advice, seek a second opinion.

Above: When iron corrodes it expands to many times its original volume; this in turn will crack surrounding masonry, sometimes resulting in severe damage to the building's fabric.

Below: Old buildings are usually riddled with cracks, some historic, some seasonal, some live. Only occasionally are cracks so serious that they render the structure unsafe, as in this example from the Orkneys. Each crack should be considered individually and treated appropriately.

Iron corrosion

Iron fixings embedded within a wall structure would generally have been 'caulked' with molten lead to form a watertight seal around the end. Over time, caulked joints often fail, letting in water and causing corrosion. This causes the iron to expand and exert a force which often leads to cracking of the surrounding stone.

If a corroded fixing is easy to locate, it should be carefully removed and, if necessary, replaced in a non-corrosive metal. For instance, iron 'saddlebars' set in stone mullion windows to support and fix leaded light windows are prone to corrosion. Where these are causing damage, they should be carefully removed and replaced. If the bar is of historic significance, it can be 'tipped' with bronze and reset.

Some iron fixings are more difficult to access, for instance iron 'cramps' which were common in the eighteenth and nineteenth centuries for fixing ashlar stone cladding to the external face of a building. In the worst case, this can require the front face to be carefully taken down and refixed with non-ferrous cramps.

Seeking further advice

When it comes to structural uncertainties, it is often advisable to appoint a structural engineer. However, engineers unfamiliar with old buildings can have a tendency to be heavy handed and to over-specify remedial repairs, leading to costly and unnecessary works. Before commissioning expensive drawings and calculations, walk around the building with your engineer to check he or she is on your wavelength. If in doubt, pay for the consultation but seek an alternative professional.

There is usually more than one solution to a structural problem, so do not be afraid to challenge any advice. Repair in situ is always preferable, keeping the integrity of the structure. It is also often cheaper to repair rather than rebuild, and a sensitive solution by the right engineer should pay for the professional fees (➡ Professional advisers, page 21).

Below: Make sure your structural engineer has experience of old building repair; if in doubt, seek a second opinion.

Roofs

Opposite: This Costwold stone roof, with random-width tiles and diminishing courses, epitomises vernacular building at its best.

Roofs contribute greatly to the overall appearance of a house. They are also one of the most important elements in preventing a building from falling into decay, so a properly designed and maintained roof is essential and should always be a priority.

Like hats, roofs provide protection from the weather. They keep out the rain and the cold, offer shade from the sun and, as with hats, are fashion statements giving clues to the status of the building. The diversity of materials used – clay, straw, stone, slate, metal, wood – results in roofscapes that give colour, texture, shape and individuality to our cities, towns and villages. They weather and mellow through exposure to the elements and, as a result of vernacular traditions, have stamped a distinctive character on Britain's regions.

The roof structure is designed to support specific materials and the type of covering will dictate the pitch, shape and strength of the roof. Some roof coverings are best suited to straight angular roofs; others offer the chance for gentle curves.

Whatever its type or style, if a roof has been poorly designed or maintained, the inevitable outcome is damage to the fabric of the building below. Roof repairs may mean just replacing the odd slate or tile but sometimes the whole roof covering must be stripped or, worse, the structure itself repaired. Whatever the case, roofs are a priority job, better done sooner rather than later.

Getting a survey

Before buying an old building, check the condition of the roof since major repairs or replacement can involve considerable costs. Ask your surveyor specifically to comment on the condition in the survey and check that internal access will be available for inspection. If not, warn your surveyor that he will need a torch and a ladder.

Below: Checking and repairing the roof should be one of the first priorities with any building, although undulating 'wobbly' roofs do not necessarily indicate a problem.

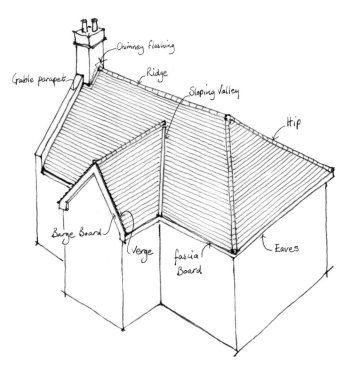

THE STRUCTURE

The way roofs were constructed was influenced by the choice of covering. Early roofs were frequently pitched much more steeply than is common in modern buildings to ensure that rain and snow could not penetrate or settle. The weight of roofing material directly dictated the design of the supporting structure.

Roofs fail for many reasons: the timber structure may have rotted or been inadequate to support the load in the first place, materials or fixings may have come to the end of their life or there might be general decay through neglect. Later alterations, such as the introduction of dormer windows, may also have weakened the original structure.

Equally, roofs can last for many hundreds of years; their wonderful undulating quality is not necessarily an indication of a defect but might be because of gentle distortion and settlement over the centuries. Care should be taken not to destroy this characteristic by unnecessary or inappropriate roofing work (➡ Timber-framed buildings, page 101).

Terrace roofs

The re-roofing of a terraced house should be a straight-forward affair and local contractors ought to be able to tackle such a project without any problem. If there is no physical break to the roof between your and your neighbour's property, it might be worth enquiring whether

Above left: the main parts of a roof.

Above: The 'mansard' roofs of this London terrace are covered in slates, some of which are decoratively shaped to add interest. Lead has been used extensively to create waterproof junctions where the various surfaces abut and repairs would need to involve careful detailing.

Below right: A large and complex roof such as this one in Dorset is expensive to maintain yet critical to the condition of the structure below.

they would like to renew their roof at the same time. There should be cost savings and the finished roof is likely to be more successful across the whole.

Roofs to bay windows in Victorian terraces are notorious for leaking, so talk through the details with your contractor and insist on quality materials and craftsmanship.

Large and complex roofs

The roof of the larger house may comprise many slopes, valleys, wells and secret gutters, making the job of re-roofing extremely complicated. For this type of roof, it is well worth using an architect or surveyor to manage the project. If certain features of the roof have always been problematic, this is the time to redesign them in a more efficient way. Try also to design access to the roof wherever you have an opportunity: this will make the job of maintenance easier in the future.

Ancient roof structures

If you have a really old roof structure, it might hold important clues about the early history of your home. For example, blackened roof timbers may indicate an open hall house, originally built without a chimney, with smoke from an open fire escaping through holes in the roof. Such features are of great historic value, so take care to preserve them. Early roofs are likely to have had a covering of oak shingles, thatch or pegged stone slates, but these may have been replaced in the last two hundred years with other materials.

ROOFING WORK

Getting your roof to function properly is the first step to preserving an old house. Forget about doing any internal work until the roof is sorted out. Roofing work is potentially dangerous and highly specialist, and not generally recommended for the homeowner to tackle, but it is important to understand the issues so that you can manage the repairs properly.

Above: Ancient roof structures tell us much about the carpentry techniques of the period as well as containing clues as to how the building has changed over time. Great care should be taken to retain as many of the timbers as possible.

Inspecting your roof

> Externally, bits of tiles or slates on the ground or in gutters are a sign of trouble. Use binoculars to inspect the roof as a whole and look for slipped and broken tiles.
> Examine the 'flashings' and 'flaunchings' at roof junctions. These are the most vulnerable parts of your roof.
> Internally, if you have a roof void or loft above habitable rooms, check whether the underside of the tiles or slates has any underlay or roofing felt. If there is, is it sound or does it have rips and tears?
> If, on cold days, there is condensation on the underside of the felt, you need to provide better ventilation to the loft space.
> If there is no roofing felt and the underside of the tiles is exposed, the last re-roofing may have been sixty or more years ago. While the roof may still be serviceable, it might need imminent attention. You can assess the condition by turning off the lights within the loft space and looking to see if any chinks of daylight are visible. If they are, wait for a heavy downpour and see if water is getting in, or leave a sheet of paper below to see if it gets wet.
> Look for rotting or worm-eaten roof timbers (➠ Timber decay, page 95).
> If slates have been refixed with lead clips, or 'tingles', this suggests that the roof covering is failing.
> If you have the odd damaged or missing slate it should be possible for a roofer to replace it relatively cheaply. Always work out why the slate has slipped. Is it just a one-off, or indicative of a bigger problem? For example, the roof may be suffering from 'nail sickness', corrosion of the fixings.

Above: Prompt replacement of broken or missing tiles is vitally important to prevent water penetration. It is a relatively easy job for a roofer.

Above: Correct scaffolding is particularly important when re-roofing: fatal accidents can occur if it is erected incorrectly. Here, a missing intermediate guardrail has created an unprotected gap.

Before the job starts, it is advisable to make a drawn, written and photographic record of features and details, including the number and layout of tile courses, to ensure that the roof can be reinstated correctly.

Your roofer should organise and be responsible for the necessary scaffolding and skips. Make sure provision has been made for wet weather, and be aware that items stored in attics and upstairs rooms are vulnerable during the work. Be prepared for the worst, especially if there is no access to inspect the condition of the timbers before the roof is stripped, as it is very difficult to assess the scope of such works in advance. The horizontal laths or battens on which the tiles are hung often serve a useful function as lateral bracing, so it may be unwise to strip a roof completely in one go. It can also be dangerous to strip a single side, since uneven loading will result.

Once the roof has been stripped, allow a gap in the programme of works for repairs. If it is a simple roof with the odd rotten rafter, your roofer should be able to tackle this for you. For a more complicated roof, it could be worth having a structural engineer on standby in case you uncover unexpected problems. Make sure the roof structure is properly repaired before putting the tiles back, and do not be bullied by your roofer into making rushed decisions. Remember, the roof is only as sound as the structure that is holding it up, and it is very difficult to carry out structural repairs once the covering is back on.

Roofs should be stripped carefully, since up to 70 per cent or more of the tiles or slates may be re-usable, depending on their condition. Make sure you are not exploited by a builder who tells you they are not, then sells them on to someone else. Try to use the materials that are salvaged to make up one complete area of roof; this can help maintain the original character of the building. Use new, but matching, materials to make up any shortfall.

If a roof is going to last and reflect the period of your home, it is vital to find the right materials. These should, wherever possible, not only match the originals but also be laid in the same way. Originally, the timber structure would have been built to support a particular weight of roof covering, so a change of material may have dire consequences. With new materials it is important to see the product before ordering, so obtain samples.

When it comes to putting the roof back, talk through the details with your roofer, particularly around chimney

Left: Many stripped tiles can be re-used when re-roofing. Sound tiles should be carefully stacked and precautions taken to prevent theft.

Right: Underlay was not originally used on roofs, but it provides an added barrier against water penetration so is worth considering when re-roofing. However, torching may be a more appropriate alternative if re-laying a roof where the underside is to be visible.

and dry. Building regulations require the provision of ventilation and roof insulation so, if your project is subject to Building Control, careful thought needs to be given to introducing such features sensitively and without damage to the structure.

Insulation

As hot air rises, a large proportion of heat is lost through the ceiling. This can easily be addressed by laying insulation between and over the ceiling joists to meet current recommended standards. It is important to retain good cross-ventilation within the roof space above the ceiling, so take care not to obstruct air flow at the eaves. The area underneath any water tank should not be insulated, since warmth rising from below helps to stop the water freezing. It is important not to forget to cover the loft hatch with insulation (➡ Insulation materials, page 191).

stacks and gable abutments. A good roofer will be happy to explain what he is doing and why. For large or complicated projects, professional advice from an architect or surveyor should be sought.

Underlays and ventilation

Modern roofs and old roofs that have been re-roofed generally have underlay or roofing felt. This is not automatically required but it does provide a secondary barrier in the event of rainwater penetrating a covering. It will catch the leaks from an odd missing tile, or channel wind-driven rain blown in between the gaps. A new generation of breathable underlays is now available which claim to be equally as waterproof from above but are designed to allow water vapour to pass from below, rather like Gore-Tex. These can reduce condensation forming on the underside of the underlay if installed correctly, although the long-term effects of such materials have not yet been tested..

With any roofing system always make sure you build in plenty of ventilation so that the timbers remain sound

Right: It is essential to give proper consideration to insulating roof spaces, which dramatically reduces heat loss and condensation. Sheep's wool is one of a number of natural fibre options and provides an alternative to mineral wool.

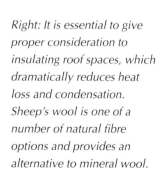

Top tip: Avoiding quick fixes

Do not be tempted to use one of the newly available systems in which foam is sprayed on the underside of the roof. This can only ever be a temporary solution and may accelerate roof failure in the longer term. The foam can restrict ventilation of the timber rafters and battens, stopping them from drying out. Eventually, this causes them to rot and need replacing; it also seriously hinders the re-use of the tiles or slates when you ultimately re-roof, making the final job considerably more expensive.

Below: Detailing at roof junctions is critical to keep out the rain. Traditionally, sloping valleys would have relied on tiles being swept round the valley (left) or laced up the valley (right). Today, it is difficult to find craftsmen who are able to execute these details; tiles are simply trimmed and butted at valleys with a lead soaker beneath. This is technically acceptable, but it impacts on the aesthetics of the roof.

TILES AND SLATES

Although tiles and slates are comparatively insignificant individually, the overall effect of a well-laid roof is extraordinary, particularly in the case of a stone roof where the individual components mesh to form intricate swept and laced valleys.

Initially, tiles and slates were laid over riven laths of oak or chestnut; by the mid-nineteenth century, sawn softwood 'battens' became a cheaper alternative. To provide insulation and prevent snow or driving rain penetrating between the tiles and slates, the underside of the roof was usually 'torched', plastered with lime or clay. This was the precursor to modern day roofing felt. In certain instances, torching may be appropriate today since it provides an attractive finish to the underside of the roof.

Wooden shingles

These are effectively wooden tiles. Oak and sweet chestnut are traditional shingling materials, though sawn cedar is now common. Each of the slices of wood has parallel sides, while the sometimes decoratively shaped lower end is thicker than the upper. Well-seasoned timber is essential and, when made by hand, the shingles are 'cleft', formed by splitting along the grain.

Clay tiles

Early clay tiles were 'peg tiles' with one or two holes to accommodate a wooden peg which hooked on to the riven laths. Later, nails were used instead. Since tiles were handmade, neither the materials nor the processes used to make them were consistent, so they were of many different shapes, shades and finishes.

During the nineteenth century, 'nibbed' tiles were introduced, enabling the tile to be hooked over the lath, rather than pegged or nailed. Towards the middle of the century, machine-made tiles began to be manufactured which were generally smoother and more regular in size. Victorian roofs often featured multi-coloured and decorative tiles.

Pantiles

Although made of the same material as plain tiles, fired clay, pantiles are very different. Larger and with a distinctive 'S' shape, designed to interlock with the neighbouring tile, they incorporate nibs that hook over the roof battens. Since the overlap is smaller than with plain tiles fewer are required, so the weight of the roof is less. The interlocking fit means that pantiles can be laid to a lower pitch; they are therefore used extensively for lean-to extensions. Their shape makes it easy to replace individual tiles without disturbing the rest of the roof covering.

By the nineteenth century, double Roman tiles were introduced. These are similar to pantiles but are larger and have two rolls rising from a flat surface, giving them better weather resistance. However, they lack the softer aesthetics of pantiles and should not be used as a substitute without careful thought.

Slates

Slate is a geological term for a type of metamorphic rock that splits along the grain. It is non-porous and frost-resistant so makes excellent roofing material. Although

Right: Handmade plain clay tiles develop an attractive patina over time. Check with your supplier that the pitch of your roof is appropriate for this kind of tile.

Right below: Pantiles are used extensively because they are suitable for both steep and shallow pitches. In this example from Norfolk, care has been taken to detail the ridge using slips of tile bedded under it.

Right: The interlocking shape of pantiles allows them to be used on a shallower pitch than a plain clay tile.

Far right: Double Roman tiles evolved from pantiles. Less appealing to look at, they are more watertight because of their regular interlocking design.

often associated with the ominous dark grey of the roofs of back-to-back terraces, its colours vary from greenish grey to blue-grey, from greens to rusty brown with tinges of pink. The most common British slates are from North Wales; other traditional examples include Collyweston, Delabole and Westmorland, to name but a few.

Originally, slates were laid in diminishing courses, with the largest at the bottom, becoming smaller towards the top. Since mass production, slates from the larger, more industrialised quarries have been laid in uniform sizes. Welsh slate in particular was employed right across Britain. It can be split into extremely thin, smooth sheets; since these are light in weight, they have the advantage of requiring a roof structure of relatively less strength. In addition, they lie flat so can be laid at a low pitch.

The quality of different types of slate varies enormously. Foreign imports of slate are available: they are much cheaper, but considerably less durable and likely to have a much shorter lifespan.

It is common to see old slate roofs coated with a combination of roofing felt and tar in a process known as 'Turnerising'. Although this may gain a few extra years from a leaking roof, it is unattractive and seriously hinders the reuse of the slate so is generally inadvisable.

Stone tiles

Certain limestones and sandstones which could be split along the grain were utilised as stone roofing tiles, although nowadays it is often hard to find suitable stone because the old local quarries have closed. The character of stone tiles varies across the country; vernacular terms for them include flags, flagstones, thackstones, slats, flatstones, stone slates, scantles and tilestones.

For stone to be used for roofing it has to be split into usable pieces. Often this was achieved through the action of frost after quarrying. The edges were then trimmed by hand and a hole was made near the top of each tile to enable the insertion of an oak peg, later a nail, to hook over a roofing batten.

Stone-tiled roofs still tend to be laid to diminishing courses, decreasing in size as they go up the roof, minimising waste by utilising all the available stone. This has the added advantage of providing the longest

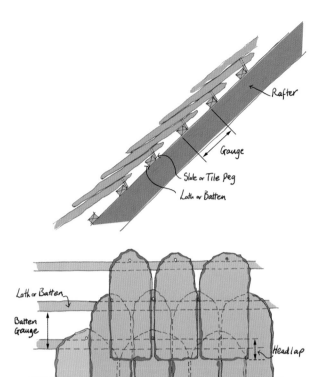

Left: Traditional stone roofs should be laid with a minimum headlap and sidelap.

headlap at the base of the roof where the rainwater runoff is concentrated. Stone-tile roofs are heavier than other kinds of roofing and the roof structure must take this into account.

Limestone roofs are generally made up of smaller tiles, allowing intricate details such as swept and laced valleys and roofs over dormer windows. The uneven texture and non-uniform thickness of the tiles create large gaps where one tile overlaps another. To prevent water penetration through the gaps, the roof is laid at a steep pitch and often bedded in mortar or 'grouted' at the joints.

Roofs of sandstone tend to utilise larger tiles and are therefore less detailed; features such as dormer windows are much harder to incorporate. Their smoother texture ensures a tighter fit, which generally allows the tiles to be laid to a shallower pitch. Try to use new rather than reclaimed tiles and slates (➧ use of second-hand materials, page 15).

Left: Laying a traditional stone roof of random-width tiles and diminishing courses is highly complex; it should only be carried out by a specialist roofer. In this example in Warwickshire, individual lead soakers will be lapped under each tile and over the 'mop stick' to form a watertight hip detail.

Right: Stone tiles are laid in diminishing courses, providing a distinctive style while minimising waste and providing added protection where there is the biggest concentration of water.

FLASHINGS AND FILLETS

One of the most common places for water ingress is at the abutment of a roof slope against a vertical wall – for instance, the junction where the chimney stack penetrates the roof covering. Regular inspection and careful repair is essential. Look for water staining inside the roof space during or after a heavy rainstorm, but check the staining is current, rather than an old problem that has been sorted out. Local failures can often be repaired fairly simply without renewing the entire roof, if the rest is sound. The three three ways to keep water out are described below.

Mortar fillet

The traditional detail for a junction is formed from lime mortar to seal the gap between the roof covering and the wall. On many old buildings, this is the only detail that will look in keeping, yet it is not the most effective at keeping water out. It may be possible to insert lead soakers under the tiles, covered with a strip of stainless steel expanded metal lath as a key to a mortar fillet above. This will give the appearance of a traditional detail without compromising water tightness. Such work should be carefully executed in hydraulic lime (NHL 5) if it is to work.

Above: A well-executed lead flashing is essential to ensure water penetration does not occur at junctions such as those around a chimney. In this instance the original flashing was simply lifted up in order to carry out repairs beneath, and then beaten back once the work was complete.

Above right: A lime mortar fillet was the traditional means of finishing a junction to the edge of a pitched roof.

Stepped flashing

If your roof abuts a brick wall, a stepped lead flashing may be the neatest and most effective solution. However, although this is ideal for a Georgian or Victorian terrace, it can look rather inappropriate on a simple vernacular building or early brickwork.

Continuous flashing

If your roof abuts irregular bonded brickwork or a stone wall, especially one built of irregular or large stones, a continuous lead flashing may be suitable. However, this requires a 'chase', or slot, to be cut into the stonework into which to fix the top of the flashing, creating a permanent scar – so be absolutely sure before taking this irreversible route. Mark the chase clearly prior to cutting and make sure it is carefully executed. These types of details have both a technical and visual impact on your building. Always discuss them in advance with your roofers and ensure that they are adequately skilled before you let them loose with an angle grinder!

Above left: Lead 'soakers' lapped under each tile and turned up the vertical wall surface are the first step in an effective watertight junction.

Above: Stepped flashing is the tidiest means of covering lead 'soakers' when used next to regular brickwork.

Right: Where brick or stonework has an irregular pattern, a continuous flashing is used to cover over the upturned soakers.

Material facts

Use the wrong roofing material and it will stick out like a sore thumb. It may even result in ongoing damage, particularly if it is too heavy or not designed for the pitch of roof. Generally speaking, a roof should be replaced with like-for-like materials.

> Traditional, natural materials such as stone and slate are guaranteed to look wonderful. While slates and stone tiles would have traditionally been sourced locally, many are now difficult to obtain as original quarries are rarely still operating. If you are able to source a good match, be sure to order well in advance.

> Handmade clay tiles are still produced in the traditional manner, but on a small scale. They contain all the undulations and imperfections of a handmade product, and look completely different from their machine-made equivalents. Most tile factories are able to make 'specials' to match missing decorative ridge tiles or a particularly unusual size.

> Salvaged or second-hand materials may not have the life expectancy of their newer counterparts. By providing a market for such products, you may also be encouraging architectural theft. Always check the provenance of any salvaged goods before you buy.

> A considerable range of imitation and machine-made roofing products is available. While these may look convincing when first laid, they tend to weather differently and do not have the enduring beauty of more natural materials.

Left: Natural slate and stone tiles often have to be finished by hand to fit their specific place on the roof, making them particularly labour-intensive to lay.

Below: The imperfections of handmade clay tiles set them apart from the machine-made equivalent.

Below: The craft of thatching developed into quite distinct vernacular traditions. In Shetland, heather was often used as a base coat with oat straw laid over the top. This is quite different from the wheat straw and water reed used throughout much of Britain.

THATCH

Thatch continued to be generally used in rural areas until the mid-nineteenth century, when the railways began to allow easy transportation of alternative roofing materials. Sadly today, our once rich and diverse thatching traditions are becoming standardised. Home-owners are all too often persuaded to re-thatch their roofs with water reed, regardless of historic precedent. Modern water reed is easier for the thatcher to lay and it is now imported in significant quantities, making it cheaper to supply. It is perceived to last longer, and is sold to homeowners on this basis, but in reality the longevity of a roof is dependent on a number of factors, including:

> The pitch: the shallower the slope the more the surface will retain moisture.
> The orientation: a south-facing elevation wears much quicker due to greater climatic change.
> Good air circulation: a thatched roof will underperform if the property is surrounded or inhibited by a tree canopy.

> The quality of the material used, which will vary from year to year in both water reed and straw.
> The skill of the craftsman.

Local traditions

Your conservation officer is an essential point of contact before you embark on a re-thatching project, and will be able to recommend craftsmen and offer advice. Thatching materials and styles vary from region to region so it is important to find a thatcher who understands the local traditions.

Materials can be broadly divided into three categories: water reed, combed wheat reed and long straw.

Water reed was traditionally used in areas with access to reed beds, typically around river estuaries or near marshland; it is often known as 'Norfolk reed'. Reed beds were carefully managed in order to farm the water reed, which was used extensively for its durability and strength. The reeds were laid on to the roof with their 'butts' down and fixed laterally by 'sways' (hazel rods),

Assessing the condition

If you are considering buying a thatched property, it is wise to take expert advice on the condition of the thatch in addition to a general survey. Try to get details of the last thatching programme.

> Are there any climbing plants growing over the roof? These could be causing damage.
> Is the rodwork damaged at the ridge or is there a gap under the netting at the apex?
> Are there any gaps around the chimney?
> Is the wire netting sound and not rusting?
> While mosses are often of concern to homeowners, they are usually harmless and protect the surface from physical damage. Some produce anti-fungal chemicals which help preserve the thatch. Unless the build-up is extreme and clearly damaging the roof, moss should not be raked off since this inevitably removes some of the weathering thatch.

Above: Thatching involves skills that have been passed down through generations; the tools have changed little and a leggett is still used to achieve a tight finish.

hidden beneath the subsequent layer. Only the bottom of the plant was left exposed, with the stem being dressed into place by a tool called a 'leggett' to form a tight finish.

Combed wheat reed was mostly used in the south-west of England and is sometimes known as 'Devon reed'. It employs a similar laying technique to water reed but the raw material is wheat straw.

Long straw also utilises wheat straw but its method of preparation and application is very different. This was once the cheapest and most common thatching method, often carried out by farm labourers. The loose straw is drawn into units of thatch called 'yealms'. These are fixed in courses to a base coat of thatch by hazel spars. The surface finish contains a mixture of ears and butts, giving a 'poured-on' appearance to the roof. The eaves and gables have surface 'liggers' (hazel rods), a technique that is not required with the other thatching methods. Traditionally, this method also called for 'rolled barges' and a flush-fitting ridge without ornamentation.

Below: A roll barge is the traditional verge detail when thatching in long straw.

Getting the job done

> Ask questions about the suitability of the new material .

> Get a comprehensive specification for the work that is proposed.

> Allow a gap in the thatching programme for any necessary repairs to roof timbers or chimneys.

> A good thatch should not require an underlay, which may cause the reed or straw to rot more quickly by holding the damp against it rather than allowing it to breathe.

> Ask your thatcher to take particular care if you have 'fleeking' or 'flecking' under your thatch. This is a thin layer of woven reed which is plastered on the underside to form a ceiling. It is easily damaged during re-thatching works.

> Traffic on a thatched roof can cause a great deal of damage: try to ensure that such things as television aerials are fixed before rethatching.

> If thatching a new extension, it is likely that a fire barrier will be required under building regulations.

> Straw roofs are normally covered by wire netting to prevent bird and vermin damage; they should be itemised in the specification. The netting should closely fit the contours of the roof and be easy to remove in the event of fire.

Above: Thatching needs to be carried out with an understanding of the roof, the materials employed and the finish required. Be sure you have thoroughly discussed the job with your thatcher in advance.

Top tip: Keep it simple

When re-thatching, craftsmen are often keen to leave their mark with fancy ridges and decoration – it is easy to fall for the 'chocolate box' effect! But remember, smaller dwellings, in particular, are unlikely to have been finished in this way. Talk through all the details with your thatcher in advance, especially ridge details.

Above: When the corrugated iron roof of this little Leicestershire farmhouse was removed and its original long straw covering reinstated, it was deliberately kept simple.

METAL SHEET
Lead

Lead sheet has long been used as a roofing material and can easily last for a hundred years when fitted correctly. Often it is used to form large flat areas and to create more complex roofs involving curved shapes such as domes. Traditionally, lead sheet was cast on beds of sand. This is still available, but from around 1900 milled lead, passed through rollers, became commonly used.

Lead sheet comes in a range of thicknesses, identified by its 'code', ranging from code 3 to code 8. When specifiying lead, it is important to use the right code for the purpose: for instance, a flat roof would be code 6 or 7, and a flashing would be code 4 or 5. The higher the code, the larger the sheet that can be laid.

Lead can easily be shaped by beating or by lead burning. Both methods have advantages and disadvantages. Beating can result in the lead being stretched and thinned, making it vulnerable to splitting. Burning will achieve a long-lasting seam but can scorch the timber substrate and has been known to cause serious fires. Contractors should be asked to take particular care when carrying out 'hot works' (➡ Preparing the site, page 29).

Lead is a complicated material to get right. Incorrect detailing, such as an oversized sheet or a poorly constructed junction, can result in expensive remedial works.

Exact and clear details for leadwork are set out in the Lead Sheet Association's manual. This should be closely followed, even for something as simple as a lead chimney flashing. It is rare to find a roofer who is skilled in leadwork, and poorly executed work is often undetected for months. If you are overseeing a roofing project yourself, check that your roofer is up to the job and compare your details with the Lead Sheet Manual. Make sure the work is inspected before the scaffold is struck or, at the very least, ask your roofer to take a photograph.

Left: Lead is visually attractive, easily worked and durable. Even so, it requires great care in its detailing and execution to ensure long-lasting performance.

Copper

Generally, copper that is failing should be replaced on a like-for-like basis since it has wonderful aesthetic and design qualities. However, in cases where copper has been used as a replacement for lead, it may be preferable to revert to the original material. Copper needs to be carefully detailed as water runoff can cause stains and streaks.

Zinc

Cheaper and lighter than lead, zinc is not nearly as durable. As well as being used as a roof covering, it has often been employed to form flashings and other junction details but its use is not recommended.

Below: As with all roofing materials, good detailing is essential with copper. The metal will quickly mellow and provides a pleasing solution when adding an extension to an old building. One of its principal advantages over lead is that it can be laid in large sheets and weighs much less.

Timber and carpentry

Opposite: Timber is an essential element of this house in West Sussex. The original wattle and daub panels have been replaced with flint and stone, reflecting the vernacular materials of the area.

Even if its presence is not immediately obvious, timber performs many important structural functions, bridging openings and holding up floors and roofs. In timber-framed houses, beams and posts are, essentially, the building's skeleton. Damp is its biggest enemy.

Early carpenters built timber-framed houses using joints held in place with pegs. Oak was predominantly chosen to form these structures because of its strength and, providing it stayed dry, its incredible durability and resilience. Trees were selected specifically for individual parts of the frame, depending on their height, girth and shape. For example, 'cruck' construction was based on pairs of curved posts inclined inwards and meeting at the top.

The timber was usually cut and shaped soon after felling when it was still green and easiest to work. Often the marks of the tools used are evident today. It was only in the highest-quality work that the timber was more carefully finished with mouldings and other details.

Proper maintenance of your house and the use of compatible materials are critical to the preservation of all timber elements, whether they are made of hard or soft wood. If decay is present it is important to identify the source of the problem and rectify the fault through repairs. Think carefully before rushing in and using chemical treatments. Avoid stripping out and replacing timber sections – you may be surprised just how sound a beam or post is, despite its outward appearance.

TIMBER DECAY

Within the last few decades, a whole industry has developed around the treatment of timber decay. Sadly, much of this involves unnecessary, expensive work which is born from a lack of understanding of the problem. Until relatively recently, it was believed that the only method of tackling beetle attack and rot was with chemicals, some of which have since been found to be highly toxic and are now banned substances. Studies have now been carried out which show that much of the decay that occurs is simply the result of timber getting damp, usually because of building defects which can easily be remedied. By resolving the defect and drying out the timber, further decay can be limited if not halted completely.

Below: Tool marks on timber surfaces tell us how the tree was originally converted; they are a link with the craftsmen of the past. These rather intangible pieces of evidence can easily be lost in the process of repair.

Left: Joinery elements such as windows and doors are vulnerable to decay if they are poorly maintained and exposed to constant wetting. Rot such as this is often indicative of a more serious building defect.

Below: Cross section through a typical mature tree trunk. When the trunk is converted into usable timber sections, any sap left on the corners is vulnerable to beetle attack.

Despite the evidence, it still remains common for timber treatment companies to work on commission. Obviously they then have a vested interest selling chemicals, and unscrupulous firms continue to specify unnecessary works that may do little to remedy the problem.

In order to grasp the nature of timber decay and beetle attack, it is critical to understand how a tree works. Wood begins as glucose but combines into cellulose and lignin. If a trunk is sliced through the middle, various layers can be identified. The outer layer is the bark; beneath that is the sapwood, the living part of the tree which conducts the water and minerals essential for growth. The sapwood has little natural durability and is vulnerable to beetle and fungal attack. After several years the sapwood converts to 'heartwood'; this is the dead part of the tree and manages the toxins within the trunk. This process adds to the durability of the heartwood and makes it particularly resilient to decay. The centre of the trunk contains the 'pith' and is less durable than the surrounding heart.

When a tree is felled for building, it is 'converted' or sawn into useful sections. Ideally, the conversion process should remove the sapwood and leave only heartwood in the final section of timber. In reality, traces of sapwood are often left on the corners of the timbers and these are vulnerable to beetle attack.

Heartwood used in buildings has a natural resilience to decay provided it is kept dry. It is only when timber is subject to moisture that the mechanism of decay can begin. In the natural environment, trees are part of the carbon cycle; they grow, fall down, rot and finally provide nutrients to other plants on the forest floor. When timber in a building gets wet, this process is replicated.

Fungal decay

Fungal decay to timber can be categorised in two principal types: brown rots (such as 'dry rot' and 'cellar rot') and white rots. Brown rots remove cellulose from wood, leaving a brown matrix of lignin behind. White rots remove the lignin as well as the cellulose, leaving the decayed wood white. The term 'wet rot', which is commonly used to describe less onerous types of rot, is misleading and should more accurately be described as anything that is not dry rot.

Dry rot

Dry rot spores are omnipresent within the air around us. Once they find a favourable habitat – a piece of timber in damp, unventilated conditions – they will settle and begin to germinate. They send out threads which develop into mycelium; these appear as white strands. Provided the damp and unventilated conditions persist, dry rot will continue in a cotton-wool-like state. However, as for any living organism, the best way to eradicate it is to cut off the source of moisture. Often a dry rot outbreak will be linked with a leaking gutter or downpipe; once the problem has been addressed, it will simply die naturally. Dry rot can be triggered in buildings that have been flooded and those damaged

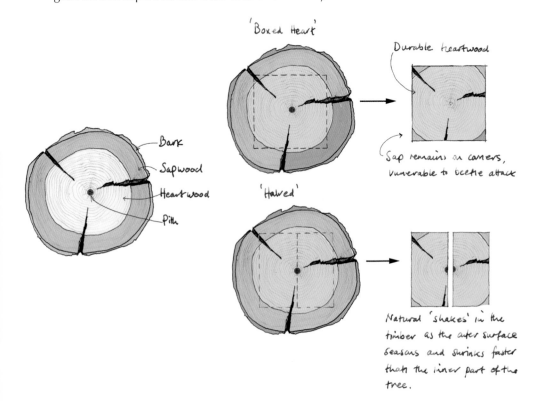

'Boxed Heart'

Durable Heartwood

Bark
Sapwood
Heartwood
Pith

Sap remains on corners, vunerable to beetle attack

'Halved'

Natural 'shakes' in the timber as the outer surface seasons and shrinks faster than the inner part of the tree.

Left: Dry rot can send out strands across inert masonry and behind plaster surfaces. These strands die naturally once the outbreak has been controlled; they do not need to be removed by stripping historic plaster.

Below: A dry rot fruiting body does not usually appear until the fungus is well established and under threat.

Brown rot: what not to do

> DON'T allow the source of moisture to persist – fix the leak!
> DON'T use specialist companies to survey the problem if they are selling a product – you are unlikely to receive impartial advice.
> DON'T remove historic plaster just because the mycelium has spread behind it – once the outbreak has been tackled, the mycelium will die naturally.
> DON'T use wall irrigation techniques to tackle the problem – these pump the wall full of liquid rather than allowing it to dry out.
> DON'T remove unaffected timber around the outbreak – provided it is dry, it will not be a suitable habitat for future spores.
> DON'T blanket-treat the area with chemicals – use chemicals, preferably boron-based, sparingly in a targeted way.
> Most importantly DON'T PANIC! Brown rot can be managed and eradicated by starving it of moisture. Far more damage can be caused by ill-advised remedial works.

by fire where the structure has become saturated due to the large quantities of water used to extinguish the blaze.

Once dry rot has been disturbed, and the environmental conditions are changed, it may make a last-ditch attempt to save itself by developing a fruiting body capable of throwing out millions of spores. Consequently, if it is not possible to dry the area immediately it is essential to monitor the outbreak. This can be achieved by creating access panels to check for secondary outbreaks. If an area is to be closed in before the outbreak has been totally eradicated, it may be worth treating it with a boron-based fungicide as a precautionary measure. Ensure that good cross-ventilation is provided to discourage future outbreaks.

Cellar rot

Cellar rot damage can be mistaken for dry rot as it thrives in similar conditions and forms a fruiting body which is not dissimilar. However, unlike dry rot, its mycelium strands are black.

Above: This outbreak of dry rot was due to a missing stop end on a gutter. While the repair to the gutter would have cost just a few pounds, the resultant damage to the building is likely to run into thousands.

White rots

White rots thrive in wetter conditions than do brown rots, typically attacking window sills and timber elements on which water settles. If left unchecked, the decay will continue to attack the timber and the rot will spread further. The good news is that white rots only affect a localised area. They can be simply resolved by cutting out all the decayed wood to a sound face and then making good with a suitable filler or, better still, piecing in a new section of timber. After repair, care should be taken to ensure that water is effectively shed or isolated from the timber to prevent the cycle from re-occurring.

Beetle infestation

Virtually every old building will have evidence of beetle attack but much of this is historic and is not a cause for concern. Look carefully at the location of any beetle holes; they will usually occur on the corner of a beam where the sapwood has been left on during the conversion of a tree to a timber section. Sapwood is particularly tasty to beetles, and is much easier to eat than heartwood, but beetles will usually stop at the interface between sapwood and heartwood without affecting the structural integrity of the timber section.

Do not be deceived by the appearance of a beam or post which has suffered beetle attack to the outer face. Medieval carpenters frequently used beams that were much larger than would be deemed structurally necessary today and oak in particular is surprisingly durable. While it may appear to be completely rotten, in the majority of cases the timber will be solid on the inside and fulfilling its structural function. Taking out timber unnecessarily is not only an expensive mistake but will result in massive disruption to surrounding fabric and the loss of historic material. Prodding with a penknife will quickly determine the condition of the timber below the surface; if there is resistance to the blade the timber may be sound even if the first few millimetres have been affected.

There are a number of different types of beetle. The two most widespread are the common furniture beetle and deathwatch beetle.

The common furniture beetle, 'woodworm', leaves exit holes of around 1.5mm and will attack the sapwood of both softwoods and hardwoods, particularly if they are in a damp environment and the moisture content of the timber is above 12 per cent. A typical roof structure may achieve a moisture content of 12–15 per cent, hence it provides a marginal environment for the beetle. Poor-quality timber which has had a large proportion of sapwood left on during its conversion is at risk of woodworm attack; floorboards tend to fall into this category due to the way they have been cut from the log. Certain plywoods, made with glues which are particularly palatable to woodworm, are vulnerable; small holes are often found in the plywood backs of wardrobes when the solid wood sides are completely untouched.

Deathwatch beetle is identified by a much larger exit hole of around 3mm. It is usually attracted to hardwoods and oak is a particular favourite, but it attacks only the damp sapwood of sound oak and stops at the heartwood. The heartwood becomes vulnerable to the deathwatch beetle if it has been previously affected by fungal attack. If this is the case, the beetle can go on to wreak havoc and undermine the structural integrity of a timber. Where deathwatch is present, it may be heard making a tapping noise during the spring emergence season. If

Above: Poorly maintained sills tend to decay much quicker than the rest of the window as water settles on the flat surface. Here, a previous attempt to cover the sill with lead has simply trapped moisture beneath it.

Right: As this section through a piece of timber shows, beetles tend to attack only the outer sapwood.

Far right: Recent woodworm activity is indicated by powdery deposits around the exit holes through which adult beetles have emerged.

Right: Deathwatch beetle, like woodworm, will generally attack only sapwood with a high moisture content. Oak is a particular favourite.

Top tip: Checking for deathwatch beetle

Beetles are lazy, and tend to reuse existing exit holes. To determine whether a beetle infestation is still active, use wallpaper glue to paste tissue paper over a group of exit holes and monitor whether they chew through the tissue during the spring.

cally alters the appearance of the timber and results in loss of the historical surface. It has often been seen as necessary as a means to 'tidy up' a beam and determine the structural integrity of the remaining timber. Such assessments can now be carried out using non-destructive techniques, obviating the need to defrass.

Defrassing is often recommended prior to the application of chemical treatments, but this is also misguided. Any chemical is far more likely to be absorbed by the open-textured frassy surface than the impenetrable heartwood beneath.

you hear this, do not rush in and try to eradicate the infestation, since your action may cause more damage than the beetle itself. The important thing is to resolve any defects that are allowing timber to get damp and then monitor an active beetle colony over time.

Monitoring beetle activity

Active beetle infestation is revealed by fine dust, 'frass', left behind by the beetles as they munch their way to the surface of a piece of timber and create their exit holes. Building works may cause vibrations that dislodge old frass; its presence does not necessarily signal current activity. The adult beetle emerges through the exit hole and starts the lifecycle again by depositing eggs. Beetles tend to exit in the spring, although common furniture beetle can continue to emerge into the summer. They usually head towards the light, so look for dead beetles around window sills and floors in front of windows during these periods. If you suspect an active deathwatch beetle colony within a dark loft space, it is possible to erect specialist light traps which attract the beetles towards them and trap them on a sticky sheet.

If you can see holes on the surface of a timber but are unsure whether the beetles are active, look carefully to see if the walls of the exit holes are dark and dirty; if they are, the attack is likely to be historic rather than live. If they are clean and light in colour, the attack is probably more recent.

Defrassing

This is the removal of a beetle-affected timber surface by hacking off back to sound wood. It usually involves the removal of the sapwood, the heartwood beneath being usually unaffected. It is a destructive process that radi-

Non-destructive testing

A non destructive test may be carried out if you are uncertain about the structural integrity of a timber element that has suffered surface decay. At its simplest, a long, fine drill bit is used to drill into the timber and assess the condition of the core. A sound core will resist the drill and make penetration difficult, while a rotten core will allow the drill to pass without effort.

For more complex situations, a company specialising in non-destructive testing will use a micro-drill. This works on a similar principal to the DIY fine-drill test but accurately records resistance via a plotter. While such a test may appear rather costly, it will usually be cheaper than unnecessary replacement. Other non-destructive inspection techniques include ultrasound scanning, fibre optic systems and, to sniff out dry rot, specially trained dogs.

Above: A micro-drill can successfully establish the condition of a structural timber with very little damage.

Four-stage holistic strategy for timber decay treatment

> Assess whether the outbreak is current or historic.
> If current, identify the source of moisture and rectify the fault through repairs.
> Assess, treat and repair the affected areas of the building's fabric sympathetically.
> Use regular maintenance to ensure that the problem cannot occur again.

Chemical treatment of beetle infestation

The 'traditional' method of dealing with beetle infestation is a blanket application of toxic chemicals, an approach which is fundamentally flawed since the chemicals rarely reach the infestation and simply result in toxins being distributed within the building. Untargeted applications such as these are far more likely to kill spiders which, as they are the beetle's only natural predator, are far more useful alive. Once timbers have dried out to below 12 per cent moisture content, the beetle will struggle to survive and numbers will decline naturally. Centrally heated buildings are very hostile environments for beetle.

If you have an active infestation of woodworm, localised and targeted application of insecticides to the affected areas can be justified, but be careful to follow the manufacturer's instructions.

Deathwatch beetle damage is a slow process, so there is no rush to resolve the problem immediately – in fact, it is impossible. Drying the affected wood is more likely to reduce the beetle population than any chemical application: the larvae are deep within the timber and any chemicals only penetrate a couple of millimetres. The most prolific beetle outbreaks are in damp, embedded timbers, such as beam ends, where there is no chance of reaching the insect.

Where chemicals are used, specialist gels and pastes with permethrin are most effective. Insecticides based on organic solvents penetrate further than water-based versions, but they are extremely flammable for some time after application and environmentally unfriendly. Permethrin-based smoke treatments are sometimes recommended but tend not to penetrate deep enough to reach the infestation.

Right: A thorough inspection by an expert in timber-framed buildings is an essential first step in understanding the problems and assessing the necessary work.

Employing a professional

If you are buying a timber-framed building, or a building with particular timber decay issues, it is critical that you employ a specialist with expertise in this area. This may be a separate report from a general survey, or you may find a surveyor who can tackle all aspects. Do not rely on information from a timber treatment company which undertakes work or sells products – they have a vested interest in specifying works and may not provide impartial advice. Mortgage providers often insist on a report from a timber treatment company and hold a retention until the work has been carried out. This practice has, for some time, led to unnecessary works and is entirely inappropriate when dealing with older buildings. What the mortgage company actually wants is a guarantee that the problem has been addressed. An impartial specialist should give your mortgage company the guarantee it requires. Most importantly, the cause needs to be identified, addressed and then monitored for a number of years. Saturated masonry may take several years to dry out, even after the source of the moisture has been removed, so any timber in contact will remain vulnerable during this period.

Decisions about what, if any, treatment is necessary should always be based on careful investigation and consideration of the facts, so resist being rushed into

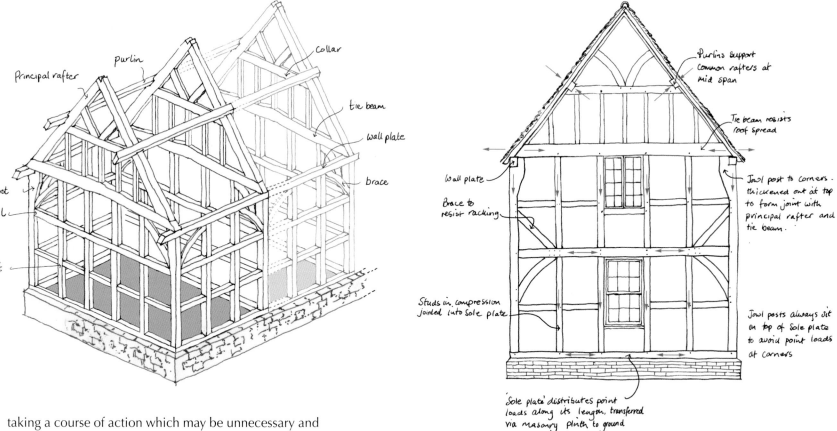

Labels on left illustration: Principal rafter · purlin · Collar · tie beam · Wall plate · brace

Labels on right illustration: Purlins support common rafters at mid span · Tie beam resists roof spread · Jowl post to corners. thickened out at top to form joint with principal rafter and tie beam. · Wall plate · Brace to resist racking · Jowl posts always sit on top of Sole plate to avoid point loads at corners · Studs in compression jointed into sole plate · 'Sole plate' distributes point loads along its length, transferred via masonry plinth to ground

taking a course of action which may be unnecessary and damaging both to the building and your pocket. It is important to remember that relying solely on chemicals to treat rot and beetle infestations will deal only with the symptoms and not the cause.

TIMBER-FRAMED BUILDINGS

The timber frame often holds clues to a building's history and original layout. It may still show the joints, peg holes and carpenters' marks where beams, long since removed, formed partition walls or door and window openings.

It is not always obvious that a building is timber-framed because the beams, along with the infill panels, may be rendered over or clad with tile hanging or weatherboarding. In Georgian times, when more classical styles were fashionable, timber structures were often re-fronted in brick or stone or, even more confusingly, clad in mathematical tiles which resemble brick.

When oak was unavailable, inferior timber was sometimes employed and plastered over to protect it from the elements. The alterations and additions made to a timber-framed building change the way it functions as a structural entity so, before embarking upon repairs, it is important to understand how your timber frame works.

Above left: Timber framing traditions vary but the basic elements are fairly generic. It is useful to familiarise yourself with the names of the parts before commencing any work on the structure.

Above right: A timber-framed house works very differently from a masonry structure. Loads are spread through a series of posts, beams and braces in tension, compression and shear. The sole plate plays a crucial role in distributing the load at the base.

Early frames usually had wattle and daub infill panels and transferred their loads entirely through the timber structure. If your building still functions in this way, try to imagine it as a skeleton, considering how each timber member is connected to the next, whether in tension or compression. However, if your frame has been heavily altered and infilled with brick, with certain elements removed and bricked up, you may find that the 'frame' no longer operates as such and is instead merely a series of timbers embedded in what is really a masonry structure. Most timber-framed buildings fall somewhere in the middle, a combination of a partially loaded frame and a masonry structure.

Repairing timber frames

Timber frames flex and settle over time, which adds to their character. Where sections of a timber frame need to be repaired, approach the job with caution and replace only what is past saving. Try to retain original elements such as wattle and daub panels or old window mullions even if, at first sight, they seem decayed and irrelevant. Such things are not always difficult to repair and it is important to stand back and appreciate their significance.

Buying a timber-framed house

It is critical to obtain a specialist survey: structural defects are often concealed and only a timber frame specialist will be able to assess the condition or make intelligent predictions of potential problems. Repairs can be costly and disruptive and should be taken into account when putting in an offer. It is important to set aside an adequate budget for such works.

In general terms, timber-framed buildings fail most commonly for these reasons:

Cement renders Where a hard impermeable render has been used, trapping dampness behind and raising the moisture content of the timber, the frame is far more vulnerable to decay. Timbers can become severely weakened over time, joints can fail and structural movement, even collapse, can result.

Change to infill panels Frames were generally constructed of four-inch wide timbers and the original wattle and daub panels would have been plastered to finish flush. In many instances, the wattle and daub has been replaced with brick infill panels. As the bricks are slightly wider than the frame, they stand proud, creating a 'ledge' on which water can collect. Over time, this water will rot the timbers from the bottom up.

Below: Understanding the condition of a timber-framed house is crucial. A coat of paint and a tin of wood filler can mask a serious problem, so do not be fooled by first appearances.

Below right: The bottom external edge of a sole plate tends to rot more quickly than the rest, especially on the exposed elevation where rain settles in the junction with the masonry plinth. Over time, the decay and softening causes it to 'roll' as the loads from above put it under compression.

Elm rather than oak Oak is very resilient to beetle attack, but sometimes elm or other less hardy species were used for the structural elements of the frame. These timbers suffer decay far more readily, particularly in damp conditions.

Inappropriate alterations Timber-framed buildings have often been altered without adequate thought to the way the structure functions as an entity. For example, where the tie beam to the base of the truss was low, it may have been cut through to create extra headroom for a doorway. Without the lateral restraint from the tie beam, the roof is liable to spread.

Rotten sole plates These are the timbers that sit on the brick or stone plinth, forming the bottom rail of the frame, also known as sill beams. The posts and studs of the frame are mortised and tennoned into the sole plate, distributing the load across the base of the building. It is common for sole plates to rot as they come into contact with moisture where they meet the plinth, especially if the ground level is higher than intended, or the sole plate has been covered with cement render. Often it is simply the bottom outer corner of the sole plate that rots, allowing the timber to 'roll'.

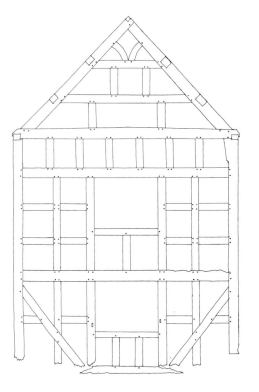
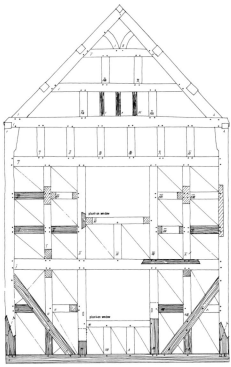

Similarly, past repairs and alterations are part of the building's history and should not necessarily be undone; beams and other elements of the fabric are best preserved in situ wherever possible, even if they no longer serve a useful purpose. Avoid stripping the structure back to its bare bones in order to establish its condition; much original and saveable fabric will be lost by such unnecessary destruction. It will also inevitably result in much extra work and cost: it can cause the structure to become unstable as cladding, infill and roof battens often provide strength to the overall structure. Where it is necessary to remove such elements, the process is best done in sections to retain the frame's overall integrity.

Movement is natural in timber and it is not always sensible to try to correct irregularities, although arresting any further movement may be necessary and wise. By attempting to force a frame back into its original position you may do much more harm than good. Likewise, to expose beams in a building where they have been hidden is not always sensible – it may result in disappointment but, far worse, it can damage the building's fabric and result in water penetration.

When embarking on anything other than minor repairs it is advisable to involve a structural engineer used to dealing with timber frames. Drawings and

Above left: Before dismantling any element of a listed building, it is essential to make an accurate record. Here, a detailed survey drawing of a timber frame provides the basis for the repair process; the elements needing work are clearly identified.

Above right: Where a timber frame is in a perilous state, temporary propping may be necessary. Repair in situ is always preferable but, in some cases, it may be necessary to dismantle and rebuild, incorporating as much of the original fabric as possible.

photographs that record the position and condition of the individual timber elements are essential to build up a picture of the overall structure. If the repair work does involve the removal of timbers, a numbering and labelling system should be instigated with each timber marked with a securely fixed plastic or plywood tag. Before removing timbers, necessary repairs and new joints should be marked up with chalk so it is clear to all involved what is required.

When a structural element of a timber frame is failing, there are three principal repair options:

Resin repairs Although these were in favour in recent years, it is now generally agreed that resins, used to consolidate or fill rotten pockets in timber elements, can actually accelerate decay. This is due to entrapment of moisture at the interface between the timber and the resin. Resins may still prove a useful tool in particular instances where only the face of the timber remains – for instance, carved or decorated timber surfaces that have rotted behind.

Metal straps Generally a far simpler repair, this uses a purpose-made metal strap to strengthen a failing joint. It is an honest repair, reversible, and can be achieved with little disturbance to historic fabric, leaving plaster and

Right: Hand-forged metal straps using a 'D' section bar are an honest, effective and reversible way of repairing a timber frame.

Below: Traditional carpentry repairs should always be carried out by a skilled craftsman. Left: the rotten timber is carefully cut away following a template of the 'scarf' joint. Centre: a corresponding joint is cut in a section of new oak. Right: once in place, the new timber sits comfortably within the old frame.

Right: Air-dried timber is ideal for small repairs and should be carefully selected from a reputable supplier.

panels in place. If a metal strap is employed, it is worth using a traditional 'D' section bar, hand-forged in mild or stainless steel. Steel should always be galvanised or painted with red oxide to prevent corrosion from the tannic acid found in oak. If steel and stainless steel are used in combination, they should be separated by nylon washers. Stainless steel nuts and bolts are the best means of fixing, to ensure the strap remains secure even if there is future timber movement.

Traditional carpentry repairs Often these involve replacing part of the timber element using a 'scarf' joint. They should be undertaken by a skilled carpenter with in-depth knowledge. For an exposed timber frame, this may be aesthetically preferable, but may necessitate the partial removal of ancient panels either side; it should, therefore, be carefully thought through.

New timber

Green oak is suitable where large areas of the frame are being replaced, but be prepared for movement and shrinkage. Infill panels are likely to develop cracks around the outside as the oak shrinks radially across its width. For smaller repairs, for example patches or scarfs, air-dried timber is more appropriate.

New timber will initially look stark against the old but, rather than staining it to match, give it time and it will take on a colour that blends in. Carving the date on new timber will be an aid to historians and those making future repairs.

Replacing a sole plate

When replacing a sole plate, builders frequently make the mistake of inserting a strip of lead directly under the new timber to protect it from rising damp. In fact, this can have the opposite effect, catching rainwater as it runs down the building and trapping it against the underside of the sole plate. It is far better to sit the new plate on a bed of lime mortar, thus allowing water to drain freely.

In many instances, rotten sole plates have been taken out and replaced with a couple of brick courses, altering the way the load is distributed. The base of the post has a very high point load, which can cause localised settlement if it is not tennoned into a sole plate. Where a sole plate has rotted, it is often necessary to replace it entirely. This may sound alarming but is a straightforward operation for a specialist craftsman.

Top: The load above is temporarily supported while the new sole plate is jacked into position.

Above: Pieces of slate or tile are driven into the gap between the sole plate and the newly built brick plinth to ensure that loading is transferred uniformly.

Right: When timber lintels are rotten they are relatively easy to replace, but the masonry above must be supported.

TIMBER LINTELS

Timber was traditionally used for lintels spanning the openings above windows and doors. Even in instances where a lintel appears to be formed of brick or stone on the outer face, timber was often used for the internal lintel. As well as being readily available and easy to work, timber lintels provided a surface for fixing laths prior to plastering around the window opening. Except in very rare instances, timber lintels were always plastered rather than exposed.

Oak lintels perform extremely well in old buildings where the wall has been maintained and the lintel has not been subjected to excessive or trapped dampness. Even softwood or elm timbers can last many years in ideal conditions, although they are not generally as durable as oak. Timber lintels can deteriorate dramati-

ROOF STRUCTURES

Ancient roof structures, especially those in oak, can last hundreds of years provided they are kept dry and are well maintained. Even so, the drip caused by a missing tile can, in a relatively short period, cause localised decay leading eventually to complete collapse. A change of roof covering, for instance from slate to concrete tile, or the insertion of a dormer window, may also result in the failure of the structure due to the extra weight.

The simplest roofs were constructed of 'ash pole rafters', whole trunks of ash, often with the bark left on. Woodworm frequently attacked the outer sapwood, so such timbers may look insubstantial but still have great strength and natural durability; they should not be replaced without good reason. By the mid-eighteenth century, many roofs were constructed from good-quality, slow-grown softwoods.

Where rafters have deflected excessively, a straight-forward solution may be to add an extra purlin or bolt a purpose-made metal plate to each side. Such strengthening works are largely reversible and preserve the original structure.

Left: Many roofs were constructed from 'ash pole rafters', whole sections of ash trees sometimes trimmed on the top surface to straighten the line. Ash is extremely resilient to decay and ideal for this situation. Here, missing ash poles are being replaced with new.

cally when coated with cement renders. In such instances, the moisture content of the timber may be increased, providing an ideal environment for wet rot, deathwatch beetle or even dry rot.

When lintels start to rot, the outer face of the timber section usually softens first, and the bearing ends are compressed under the load. If a building is rendered, this may show up as a crack in the render or, internally, as a crack to the plasterwork. Do not assume that a lintel which has started to rot a little will automatically need replacing. It is critical to dry out the lintel by removing any impervious paints or cement renders before assessing the timber. This may be done with non-destructive testing techniques.

If it is necessary to replace a lintel, consult an engineer used to specifying wood. A good option in most cases is semi-dry oak. There may be special reasons to use precast concrete or steel, but these may result in problems making good around the window, or cause a 'cold bridge' (where there is no insulation between the inner and outer surfaces) in a thin wall with the result that condensation occurs.

FLOOR STRUCTURES
Ground floors

Many Georgian and Victorian houses were constructed with suspended-timber ground floors, rather than the solid flag or tile floors of earlier times. These consist of timber joists resting on 'sleeper walls' to raise them off the damp earth, supporting floorboards on top. They were designed with air grilles, front and back, to provide underfloor ventilation to keep the timbers dry.

Suspended timber floors fail for several reasons:
> Debris build-up in the sub-floor void, creating a bridge for moisture between the damp ground and the timber structure.
> Very damp ground, so moisture rises via capillary action through the sleeper walls to the timbers.
> Air grilles becoming blocked, eliminating the through draught which keeps the timbers dry.
> The ground level being built up on the outside so water tracks through the walls, rotting the joist ends.

Where such damage is serious, there is usually little option but to dismantle the floor, clear out the sub-floor void, make good the air grilles and replace the joists. It is worth inserting a plastic isolating membrane between

Above: Adequate ventilation is vital below suspended timber ground floors, so make sure air grilles are kept free of obstructions.

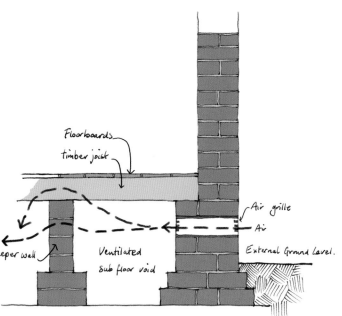

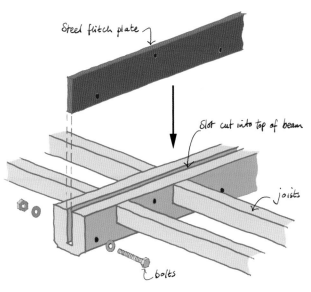

Far left:Typical detail for a suspended timber floor. Air flow enters via the grilles and runs between the joists over the sleeper walls.

Left: A steel flitch plate can sometimes be inserted into deflecting beams to provide extra stiffness. In this case, the slot has been stopped short of the bottom of the beam to conceal the flitch from the underside.

the sleeper wall and the underside of the joists to prevent future problems. Insulation can be fitted between the joists. If boards are carefully lifted, a good proportion of them may be reused.

Upper floors

Upper-floor structures usually consist of joists and one or more beams to reduce the span. Ideally, joists should run parallel to the rafters and be built into the external wall at one end to provide additional lateral restraint.

It is common for beams to sag under their own weight, and dip quite alarmingly in the middle of a floor. Many floors will actually 'tighten up' when such movement takes place, and it may not be necessary to do anything other than build up the legs of your bed on one side! If beams are showing signs of stress through cracking across the grain, a structural engineer may need to advise and specify repairs. It is sometimes possible to strengthen beams with minimum disturbance, using 'flitch plates'. Boards are lifted to access the top of the beam, a slot is cut down the centre, a template created, then a steel plate is manufactured so that it can be inserted and bolted through from either side.

Failing joists

Cracks in ceilings can indicate weakness in the floor structure above. This may be due to inadequately sized joists for that particular span causing the floor to be unduly springy, or a stress crack across a joist. It is not unusual to find that an electrician or plumber has cut

notches to the upper faces of joists in order to lay cables or pipes, dramatically weakening them. These issues should be investigated from above by carefully lifting boards rather than disturbing an original ceiling. Problems can often be resolved by strengthening the existing joists with metal straps to improve stiffness, or by fitting additional joists.

Rotten beam ends

Traditionally, beams were built directly into external walls. Where a wall has been poorly maintained and has become saturated, the bearing end is exposed to a high moisture content and will consequently rot over time. Once it is rotten, it is necessary to re-establish a structural connection with the wall. This may be achieved with a purpose-made steel 'shoe'. Alternatively, in visually sensitive situations, a threaded stainless steel bar within a special fabric sleeve may be inserted from the outside. Once in place, the sleeve is filled with resin to form a tight friction connection between the timber, the bar and any masonry.

Floorboards

Old floorboards are likely to have a rich patina that is impossible to replicate once destroyed, so endeavour to preserve them, particularly if you are lucky enough to have original oak, elm or other hardwood boards.

Grit and dirt quickly scratch a wooden floor, so sweep or vacuum regularly and make sure there are adequate mats at exterior doors. Sanding or over-zealous

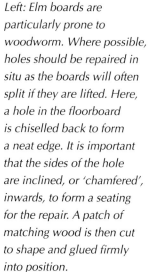

Left: Elm boards are particularly prone to woodworm. Where possible, holes should be repaired in situ as the boards will often split if they are lifted. Here, a hole in the floorboard is chiselled back to form a neat edge. It is important that the sides of the hole are inclined, or 'chamfered', inwards, to form a seating for the repair. A patch of matching wood is then cut to shape and glued firmly into position.

scrubbing not only destroys the surface patina of boards, altering their colour and character, but may also reveal an inner worm-ridden mess resulting from past beetle infestation which will be difficult to consolidate.

Lifting boards is a major cause of damage. The work should be done by someone who understands the importance of the floor; it may be worth getting a carpenter to lift boards gently before your electrician or plumber arrives! Non-powered hand tools should always be used. When cutting or nailing, beware of any pipes or cables that may be running underneath.

When temporarily lifting floorboards, number them with chalk and record their position on a plan. Where possible try to avoid the repeated lifting of boards by different trades when services are installed. If they are likely to be taken up again in the future, boards are best screwed down with brass screws rather than nailed. This option should also be considered when working above delicate plaster ceilings which might be damaged by hammering.

Floorboards should be laid using special 'cut' floorboard nails to prevent squeaks. Employ temporary wedges to ensure that boards are butted as closely as possible, to minimise gaps later.

Repairs

As with all work to old buildings, it is preferable to repair rather than replace original materials. By using the appropriate species of wood and matching the grain pattern, very satisfactory repairs can be made to individual floorboards without losing more than the minimum amount of original timber.

Beetle infestation may not necessarily weaken floorboards so much that they have to be replaced. A weakened board can be strengthened from below by screwing battens to the joists, while split boards can be glued and cramped back together. New timber may be carefully spliced in to make repairs to a broken end, corner or edge.

Gaps between floorboards can be filled with thin slivers of matching timber. Alternatively, papier mâché or lengths of string stained to match and carefully glued into place are effective. It is generally inadvisable to cure gaps by lifting all the boards and refixing them closer together: this will inevitably cause damage and the sub-floor structure will be weakened if too many boards are removed at once.

*Above: Original floorboards
need to be treated with care
if they are to retain their
character, so think twice
before attempting to lift,
sand or clean them.*

Solid floors

Opposite: The beauty of an old floor is impossible to replicate. Here, the wear patterns, texture, random nature and mellow colour of the stone all enhance the building's timeless quality.

The worn surfaces of an original flagstone, brick or tiled floor are often formed over decades if not centuries and have a character that cannot be replicated. Yet original solid floors have long been disregarded, altered or replaced with little thought to the resulting problems and aesthetic effect.

Beaten earth floors continued to be laid in humble vernacular dwellings well into the early nineteenth century. These were dusty and tended to break up with traffic, not to mention their tendency to turn to mud when they got wet. In areas where suitable stone was available in large flat pieces, flagstones were adopted by those that could afford them.

In the eastern counties, clay 'pamments' were common and, by the eighteenth century, paving bricks were available throughout the country. Tight-fitting marble slabs of contrasting colours in chequerboard patterns were often employed in elegant entrance halls. Slate was another popular flooring material and, being impervious to water, was ideal in cellars and basements. In Victorian times, quarry, geometric and encaustic tiles, which harked back to the intricate designs found in medieval monasteries, became common.

An irrational fear of damp has resulted in the loss of many such floors, even though they were often dry, serviceable and beautiful. The real issue with original solid floors relates to our expectation of performance – they are difficult to keep hygienically clean and are totally incompatible with fitted carpets. But if we really want a

traditional farmhouse kitchen, historic stone or clay tiles with all their imperfections are part of the package.

UNDERSTANDING AN HISTORIC FLOOR

Before rushing in and disturbing an original floor, it is essential to understand how it works and to consider what, if anything, needs to be done. It is unlikely that whatever replaces it will ever look as good or function so well in relation to the rest of the house; your actions may result in difficult-to-resolve problems in the future.

Before the mid-nineteenth century, bricks or flagstones were laid directly on the earth, possibly with a little sand for levelling; smaller tiles had a lime mortar bedding to hold them in place. The houses in which they were laid had no damp-proof courses in either walls or floors, and moisture was free to evaporate within the structure. Provided the internal floor level was raised a few inches above the external ground level, and so long as the ground was not marshy or permanently saturated, the floor would remain relatively dry. Even on clays, which are slow to drain, any slight ground moisture

Below: These enormous blue slate flags in a cottage in South Wales were locally quarried from the Preseli Mountains.

Bottom: Pamments were an alternative to flags where suitable stone was not available. Evidence of historic repair adds to this floor's interest and beauty.

Above: Traditionally, solid floors were laid on the earth using just a little sand or lime mortar for levelling. No damp proof membrane was incorporated and the floor was able to breathe.

Right: The previous owners of this old cottage had layered the floor with a variety of modern coverings. When the rubber-backed carpet was lifted, modern tiles were discovered laid over lino from the 1950s. Under this sandwich of impermeable materials the original 300-year-old pamments were discovered. After removal of the modern layers, the floor was allowed to dry out and simply scrubbed with mild detergent to restore its beautiful finish.

under the floor during periods of heavy rain would readily evaporate through gaps between the tiles or flags.

Why 'problems' occur

Problems occur with solid floors when modern linoleum, plastic floor coverings and rubber-backed carpets are introduced. When laid directly over old floors, or over a concrete screed applied to an old floor surface, they have disastrous consequences. Unable to escape, moisture sweats on the underside of the impermeable coverings, mould forms and the smell of damp frequently permeates the room.

In reaction to this, it is commonly believed that an original floor laid directly on earth is a disaster waiting to happen. Many solid floors have been down for centuries without any problem, yet homeowners are persuaded to lift them, excavate several inches down, lay a plastic damp proof membrane (DPM) and a thick slab of concrete. Sometimes attempts are made to re-lay the original flagstones but it is unlikely that the finished surface will ever recapture the patina and undulations created by centuries of foot traffic.

Even after this work is complete, there can be knock-on effects which can cause far greater problems. If the earth beneath the floor is at all damp, it will probably get

damper after excavating several inches down. By laying a plastic membrane over damp earth, the moisture is forced along the underside of the DPM to the first point at which it can evaporate, usually the walls. As walls to older houses contain no damp-proof course, the insertion of a plastic membrane can cause rising damp.

In addition, excavating down to lay the new floor might require going below the footings of the house. This can result in structural problems by undermining the base of the wall.

Dealing with damp

In an old house that has escaped major 'modernisation', the ground floors might be covered with layers of lino and carpet. By simply lifting these modern coverings you should be able to establish whether there is an original solid floor laid on the earth. If there is, and damp appears to be present, try to resolve the problem simply by addressing the potential sources before resorting to invasive and costly work.

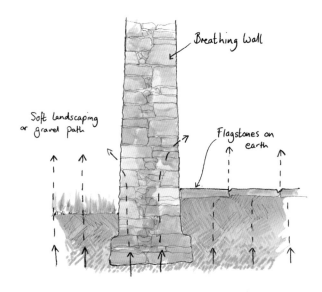

Soft landscaping or gravel path

Breathing Wall

Flagstones on earth

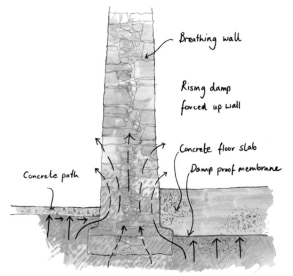

Breathing wall

Rising damp forced up wall

Concrete floor slab

Damp proof membrane

Concrete path

Ground moisture concentrated at base of wall

Far left: In a breathing building with a solid floor, it is critical to keep external ground levels lower than the internal floor level. Provided the site is reasonably well drained, the floor should remain dry without a damp proof membrane. If a small amount of moisture is present under the floor it will readily escape through the joints in the tiles or flags.

Left: When renovating an old building, many builders feel it is necessary to lift old floors, lay a damp proof membrane and a concrete slab. But digging down to wetter earth then covering with an impermeable layer often forces moisture along the underside of the floor to escape up the wall to a point where it can evaporate. The problem is further exacerbated if hard surfaces, such as concrete paths, go right up to the external wall; they can cause rising damp where none existed before.

Localised damp

A localised patch of damp on a floor may be resolved relatively easily without lifting the surface. It is likely to be due to:

> A fracture in an underground clay drain pipe running close to or under your floor. This can be checked with a drain survey and camera.

> A build-up of earth to the outside, raising the external ground level above the internal floor level.

> A defect at the base of the wall, maybe a leaking downpipe or gulley, or open joints in the masonry.

> Water and heating pipes bedded below a floor, a potential source of leaks which can be notoriously difficult to track.

> Condensation, particularly on cold floors in unheated rooms.

When you uncover a solid floor there may well be a smell of damp initially; this is likely to be due to the moisture that was trapped under the covering. By thoroughly ventilating the room the original floor may dry out naturally. Observe the floor during periods of heavy rain and visually assess whether dampness is rising. A little darkening of the joints between the tiles or flags is not necessarily a cause for concern, depending on your final floor finish and use of the room.

Solid floors on earth need to breathe; fitted carpets on rubber underlays are totally incompatible with them. A rug or sisal-type matting, leaving a margin of bare floor around the perimeter of the room, is ideal, provided the floor is relatively dry. Once your house is heated and ventilated, any slight rising moisture should simply evaporate.

Left: The joints of this original flagstone floor have been pointed in a hydraulic lime mortar to allow moisture vapour to escape. Loose rugs, without rubber backing, can provide added comfort.

MAINTAINING BRICK AND STONE

Most clay tile and flagstone floors can be cleaned using a mild detergent (such as washing-up liquid) diluted in hot water and scrubbing with a stiff bristle brush. Avoid flooding the floor with excess water, and mop up and rinse as you go.

Ideally, old floors should be protected during building works, but for occasional stubborn lumps of mortar or plaster stuck to the surface a dilute hydrochloric acid ('brick acid' or 'patio cleaner') may help. Always carry out a trial first and take extra care not to damage softer types of stone which react adversely, particularly soft limestone tiles. If neutralisation of chemical cleaners is required, ensure that this in done and follow the manufacturer's instructions. Never use abrasive cleaning methods.

To bring up the colour of the stone or tile and to keep dust at bay, a light smear of beeswax may be worth experimenting with. Avoid smearing beeswax over the joints as this is where evaporation takes place. Excessive wax can trap dirt, darken floors and form a slippery surface. Be wary of modern sealants as they may inhibit the floor's ability to breathe, which can hasten decay. Always research the product and experiment on a small area first.

Particular care should be taken when cleaning or polishing floors made of marble. It is a vulnerable stone and can be damaged even by water.

Salts

Salt efflorescence can occur on solid floors, particularly where excessive moisture has been present, where salted foodstuffs have been stored, or in places where animals have been housed and their urine has soaked into the floor. Salts may appear as white staining. If they are 'hygroscopic', they may draw moisture to them and cause the floor to appear damp. While this is unsightly, it is usually harmless. Loose salting can generally be brushed or vacuumed off. Avoid washing salts off since this is likely to redissolve them and send them back into the floor. In severe cases, poulticing may be considered, in which a paste carrying a reactive chemical is applied to the floor to draw out the salts. This is usually carried out by a specialist company.

Re-laying

In some cases there may be no alternative but to re-lay a stone or brick floor, but damage is likely to occur to the existing materials as they are lifted.

If individual stones or bricks are rocking, they can be rebedded in coarse sand or a dab of hydraulic lime mortar. Where an entire floor has to be re-layed, clearly number each brick or stone with chalk and record its position on a plan. Where possible avoid disturbing the existing substrate, but where this has to be replaced build up a good thickness of hardcore and then re-lay the floor on a new bed of sand.

Many solid floors are not pointed; if pointing is required, hydraulic lime mortar should be used to allow the evaporation of moisture.

Above: Old floors can last for centuries and these Cumbrian flags are remarkably durable. Cleaning should not normally require anything more than warm soapy water, but be sure not to flood the floor in the process.

Right: When relaying bricks or pamments, try to butt them up as closely as possible to minimise gaps.

TILES

Quarry, geometric and encaustic tiles are produced from clay, the last inlaid with clays of different colour to create designs. These are still produced today and a good tile supplier will advise on how to lay them, the adhesives to use, cleaning solutions and suitable floor finishes. If you are trying to match original tiles, take an existing tile or a photograph and the exact dimensions with you.

Tiled floors generally require little maintenance, just regular sweeping or vacuuming to remove grit that may damage the surface. Warm water or specialist tile cleaner may be used sparingly to remove surface dirt, but it must be carefully rinsed off. Never soak a tiled floor. Avoid household detergents, scouring powder, caustic soda and hydrofluoric acid.

In Victorian times, tiles were largely untreated and over time took on a sheen brought about by the polishing action of wear. Even so, unglazed tiles may be subject to staining, so consider one of the specialist products designed for these tiles that are now available. Exterior tiling should not be sealed as this can reduce its resistance to frost.

The most common problem with these floors is that individual tiles become loose or broken. Usually, they can be prized out carefully with a knife and re-layed with appropriate adhesive.

More extensive damage is usually due to the break-up or movement of the substrate into which the tiles are bedded. It is important to ascertain the reason for the deterioration and to fix the problem before attempting to re-lay the tiles. The reinstatement of large areas of an original floor is a skilled job and should be left to specialists.

Top right: Geometric tiles were generally left untreated, but should be regularly swept or vacuumed to remove grit.

Below right: Encaustic tiles were often mixed with plain geometric or quarry tiles to create patterns.

Left: Encaustic tiles were mass-produced and extensively used in Victorian and Edwardian terraces.

Top: 'Plaster' floors, also sometimes known as limeash, were a common finish in areas close to gypsum quarries.

Above: The construction of a plaster floor can be clearly seen from below: water reed was laid over the joists to form shuttering for the plaster, which was trowelled on wet. Once dry, it formed a rigid slab.

Above right: Rotten floorboards should be carefully removed and, ideally, replaced with like-for-like materials.

PLASTER AND LIMEASH FLOORS

Dating back at least to medieval times, plaster (limeash) floors continued to be used in houses and agricultural buildings into the early twentieth century; they are particularly common in the Midland counties close to gypsum deposits. Their exact composition varies, but they generally contain burnt gypsum, aggregates, lime and ash from the kiln. The wet mix is laid over laths, boards or reeds, floated to form a slab which dries to a high strength. Often used on upper floors, probably as a cheap alternative to floorboards, they provided a degree of fire separation between the house and the roof.

Such floors have a similar appearance to concrete and, for this reason, many have been unwittingly destroyed. It is usually possible to tell the difference by looking at what the floor has been laid on, and a gentle tap should cause a plaster or limeash floor to 'ring'. Those that remain usually incorporate patches of more recent concrete repair.

Limeash and plaster floors can be repaired, or re-laid from scratch. This is usually specialist work which ideally requires some analysis of the original material. Certain lime suppliers sell a dry product that can be mixed with water to carry out small patch repairs.

MODERN SOLUTIONS

When laid in old buildings, concrete floors incorporating a damp proof membrane may, as has been explained, have the effect of forcing moisture to the walls, resulting in low-level damp problems. Various alternatives to solid concrete slabs will not upset the moisture equilibrium of the building in this way.

Suspended timber floors

If you have a rotten suspended timber floor, it is better to use a like-for-like timber solution rather than be tempted to replace it with a concrete slab. This is one system where fitted carpet is compatible (➡ Floor structures, page 106).

Beam and block floors

Standard in new-builds, these are a good compromise when adding an extension to an old building if a lime-crete floor is not suitable. Unlike a basic cast concrete slab incorporating a DPM that can send moisture to the walls, a beam and block floor is constructed with a ventilated sub-floor void. Precast concrete beams carry concrete blocks, over which insulation is laid. Under-floor heating can be incorporated within the screed as normal.

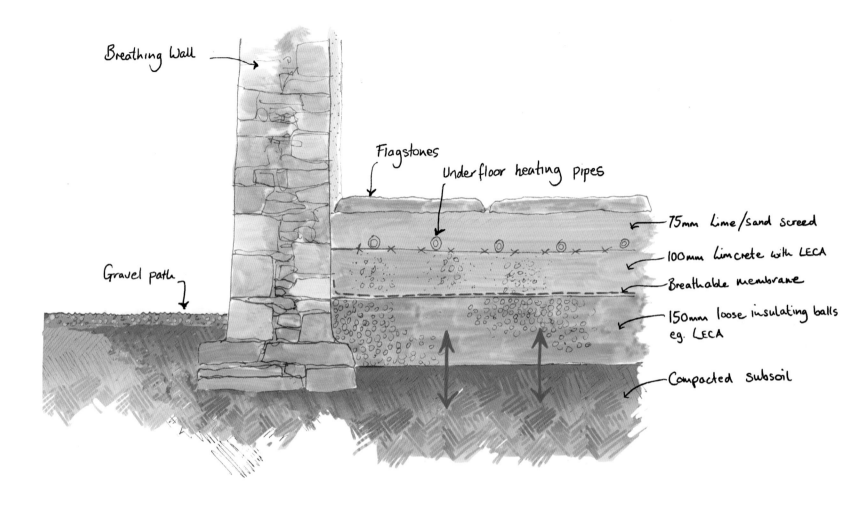

Breathing Wall

Flagstones

Underfloor heating pipes

75mm Lime/sand screed

100mm limecrete with LECA

Breathable membrane

150mm loose insulating balls eg. LECA

Gravel path

Compacted subsoil

'Limecrete' floors

Where a solid floor solution is preferred, a 'limecrete' floor is ideal. A mixture of hydraulic lime, sand and insulating material, its principal advantage is its ability to resist rising ground moisture without the need for a plastic membrane. It can be designed to meet building regulations by incorporating adequate insulation in line with current standards; it is also compatible with under-floor heating.

Check various materials suppliers and ask for a detailed specification. If you have to dig down to accommodate the floor slab because you have limited headroom, you should consult a structural engineer as this could disturb your footings.

Once the floor is laid, it can be walked upon within hours, but always allow at least four weeks for it to dry before laying a final finish.

Above: The first layer in a limecrete floor is made up of loose 'balls' of insulating material. This should be non-porous, and aerated and lightweight for maximum insulation. It acts as a sump in which the ground moisture can rise and fall without being drawn up by capillary action. Limecrete is trowelled on over a geotextile and can take cables or pipes for underfloor heating.

Laying a limecrete floor

1. Prepare the earth base ready to lay the floor. This may mean digging down, ideally 350mm minimum below finished floor level, but this varies according to the design of the floor. Ensure the surface is level and compacted. Set pegs into the ground to indicate the levels of the layers.

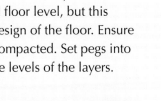

2. Lay 150mm of suitable loose insulating material, such as LECA (lightweight expanded clay aggregate).

3. Lay a breathable membrane, such as building paper or geotextile, above the loose balls. Cut around the pegs – this is not a vapour membrane and will not be damaged if it is breached.

4. Using a cement mixer, prepare the limecrete. This is usually 1 part hydraulic lime (NHL 3.5) to 1 part sharp well-graded sand to 2 parts lightweight insulating material. Mix to a porridgey consistency, not too wet. Be sure to use goggles once the water is added and the mixer is turning.

5. Lay large boards as temporary load-spreaders to access the floor, then barrow in the mix.

6. Trowel on the mix to form a 100mm thick slab. Those used to lime may work bare-handed, but gloves are recommended. Goggles should also be worn in case of splashing.

7. Check the floor for levels using a straight edge, working between the marks on the pegs.

8. For underfloor heating, lay the pipes or cables over the limecrete layer. Once they have been tested, lay hydraulic lime screed over the top. Set the top layer of flags or tiles in a weak hydraulic lime mix.

Chimneys, flues and fireplaces

The introduction of the chimney dramatically changed the layout of the house. Since the sixteenth century, the chimney and fireplace have evolved to be ever more efficient, and were frequently altered to reflect fashion. Understanding how your fireplace works is the key to maximising its performance.

In early homes, fires were lit on a hearth in the centre of the ground floor and smoke simply escaped through louvres, or even just gaps in the roof covering. Higher-status domestic buildings were called 'open halls'. These were more than a single storey in height, with the central section open from the ground floor to the roof to provide an uninterrupted path for the smoke. As houses evolved, means of channelling the smoke upwards and through the roof were incorporated. These simple smoke bays and hoods developed into the flue and chimney arrangement we recognise today.

Early inglenook fireplaces were designed to burn large logs. In smaller houses, the fireplace would also have been used for cooking, incorporating a bread oven to the side. These large openings were extremely inefficient: they required a wide flue, so that much of the heat was lost up the chimney.

Coal was not commonly used for domestic heating and cooking until the eighteenth century. Cast iron hob grates were developed for burning coal and their decorative surrounds became known as 'chimney pieces'.

Poorly maintained fireplaces and flues remain one of the principal causes of fires in old buildings. Regular inspection and maintenance are the key to averting disaster.

FLUES

The 'flue' is simply a funnel that transports smoke from the fire to the external environment. It relies on the warm air generated by the fire rising upwards to transport combustion products safely to a place where they can be dispersed. Chimneys were almost always constructed of brick or stone. Traditionally, flues were lined with a coat of lime plaster and cow dung, 'parging', which created a smooth internal surface to prevent leaks and which minimised any ledges where soot might build

Opposite: As well as serving a practical purpose, chimneys are an important architectural feature, as in this Lutyens house in Surrey. Care needs to be taken that they function correctly and are maintained appropriately on the outside.

Below: Fireplace design evolved rapidly throughout the eighteenth century. Here, the original large opening has been closed in with a variety of later insertions.

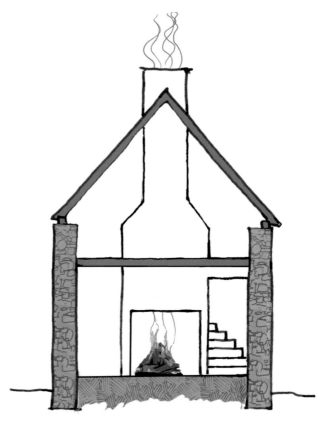

Left: In early dwellings, a fire was lit in the centre of the room and smoke simply escaped through the roof. The invention of chimneys revolutionised the internal arrangement of the house. Once a way of channelling smoke had been developed, upper floors could be inserted, necessitating the provision of stairs.

Ancient clues

If you own a very old house, you may find traces of an earlier 'open hall' that existed before the chimney was inserted. Look at the underside of the roof timbers for signs of smoke blackening. This is a deposit of black soot on the surfaces where the smoke collected before escaping through the roof. Occasionally, smoke blackening can be found on the underside of ancient thatch where early layers have remained undisturbed.

Above: This medieval roof structure retains soot deposits, indicating its early form as an open hall prior to the insertion of a chimney.

Left: Early chimneys were often built in an ostentatious manner to demonstrate wealth. Later they became features of architectural expression. This house in County Antrim was designed in the Arts and Crafts style by Clough Williams-Ellis.

up. A single chimney usually contains more than one flue, divided by 'withes' or 'mid feathers' of brick, slate or stone. These deteriorate, or are damaged over time by careless chimney sweeping, allowing the smoke to leak into an adjacent flue.

Flues fail for two principal reasons. First, cracks or holes may develop, allowing combustion gases to escape into rooms or roof spaces: this is a danger to human health, particularly carbon monoxide, which is deadly. Secondly, tar can build up over a period of time on ledges inside the flue: it may ignite and cause a chimney fire. This is particularly prevalent where unseasoned timber is used for burning, generating excessive tar during combustion. If it gets damp through rainwater penetration or condensation, this deposit of tar will bleed through the walls and cause ugly staining to appear within the room.

It is important to check the condition of your flue before you use it, especially if it has been redundant for a number of years. Get it swept by an experienced

Top: A smoke pellet is an easy way to test your flue for leaks.

Above: If possible, seal the top of individual flues when testing with smoke pellets.

sweep. This will ensure that there are no nesting birds and will also clear it of any loose soot deposits. If your sweep brings down a lot of loose material, it is a good indication that your flue is in poor condition.

Test the flue for airtightness using a smoke pellet (available from plumbers' merchants). Create a draw initially by lighting a loosely crumpled sheet of newspaper and holding it at the base of the flue. Light the smoke pellet and place on the hearth; then look in your upper rooms and roof space to check for any leaks. If you have scaffold access to the top of your chimney stack, seal off the apertures to increase the pressure of the smoke within the flue.

A chimney 'balloon' will stop the draught down a chimney when it is not in use. Available from fireplace shops, they are inflated when installed and deflated for removal.

Woodburning and multi-fuel stoves

If you have an inglenook that is inefficient or does not draw properly, a woodburning or multi-fuel stove may be a solution. Never use a stove in an existing chimney without a properly installed flue liner, and always fit a rain hat to the top of the stack to prevent rainwater corroding the appliance. Take extra care if installing a stove in a thatched building. Extreme heat is generated within the flue, so temperature sensors linked to an alarm system should always be fitted.

Stoves are a good option in a building with no existing fireplace or chimney, since a stove pipe can be fitted relatively easily with little disruption to the original fabric.

Left: Flues were usually incorporated within the thickness of the wall; here, they project externally, revealing how the flues from two separate fireplaces converge into a single stack.

Right: Be aware that stoves can get very hot. They should always be installed by an experienced fitter, incorporating a suitable flue liner.

Top left: A flexible stainless steel flue liner is a reversible option that minimises damage to the chimney.
Top right: The liner is carefully lowered down the chimney from above.
Above left: Once the liner is in place, the opening around it is closed off and the pot is bedded in lime mortar. The adjacent flue is capped, as it is no longer in use, but air grilles are installed in the stack wall for ventilation.
Above right: The top of the chimney is flaunched, using hydraulic lime mortar. The 'dummy' pot is packed with mortar to prevent it filling up with water.

Lining flues

If your flue and chimney are in good condition, there is no reason why they cannot be used safely with a working grate or open fire. A faulty flue may have to be lined if it cannot be repaired from the outside. A solid-fuel stove should never be used without a modern lining, because of the heat of the combustion gases and the risk of fire.

There are two principal systems for retrospective chimney lining. The first uses poured lightweight concrete, cast around either an inflated 'sock' or a flexible liner. Heavily marketed, it may sound like a good option but is generally not advisable for use in old buildings: it is irreversible and can go disastrously wrong. Poured concrete will find its way into every cavity and crack, and cannot be controlled once the pour starts. A rigid concrete flue can also impact on the structure of an old building, which may flex or move seasonally. The long-term effects of such an addition are at best unpredictable and at worst disastrous.

As with so many repairs to old buildings, the gentle, reversible option is a much safer path to take. The second system meets these criteria: a flexible, stainless steel flue liner. Double-skinned for solid fuels and single-skinned for gas fires, a liner is relatively simple to fit. Basic advice includes:

> Get your flue thoroughly swept before any works start.
> Organise proper access, ideally scaffolding – the liner will need to be fitted from the top down.
> Choose a liner with the correct diameter for your appliance.
> Make sure you fit it the right way up.
> Ideally, the liner should be insulated, either with a loose fill poured in from the top or with specially designed 'sleeves'.
> Remember to fit a rain cap – unlike a masonry-lined flue, the wall of a metal liner will not absorb rainwater.

An inglenook with an open hearth needs a wide-diameter flue liner, ideally 300mm minimum; such liners are extremely expensive. If you are installing a woodburning stove, a 150mm or 200mm liner is generally required, according to the appliance. A stainless steel flue liner should last for ten to fifteen years, depending on how regularly the fire is lit. Greater care should be taken when sweeping a liner, using a gentler brush.

CHIMNEYS

The word 'chimney' refers to the structure which surrounds one or more flues. It may be an integral part of the building or added later as an independent structure.

Above the roofline, a chimney will require re-pointing or re-rendering more regularly than the rest of the external walls, due to its exposed location. Keep a regular check on your stack with a pair of binoculars. Allow time and money for maintenance works during a roofing contract while there is a scaffold for access. As well as the action of weather on the outside, combustion gases from an unlined flue can also attack mortar joints over time. Hydraulic lime is ideal for re-pointing a stack (➡ Hydraulic limes, page 44).

The section of chimney just below the roofline is prone to spalling and decay, particularly in older buildings where no damp-proof course is built in. This is due to water from the exposed part of the stack draining

Restoring a cast iron fireplace

Fireplaces in Georgian and Victorian houses that have been disused for many years can usually be brought back into service with a little care and effort, provided the flue has been tested to ensure a fire can burn safely.

Check that the fireback is operational and inspect it for cracks or other damage. If you have to remove the fire surround, never force it off the wall; look for the lugs and screws which are generally buried behind the plaster on either side.

Traditional style graphite-based grate polish can be used to 'black lead' cast iron fire surrounds which have been stripped of paint. When burnished hard with a soft, dry cloth, this leaves a lustrous black finish. Alternatively, stove paint provides a matt black finish and is specially designed to withstand high temperatures.

Specialist fireplace shops will advise on repairs and generally supply new firebacks and other materials, such as the fireproof rope and cement used to seal gaps around the fire surround.

Above: Graphite-based polish gives a good finish on stripped cast iron fireplaces.

Above: These ancient Scottish stacks would unnerve many an engineer: they are tall and slender and pose a potential safety risk to the public. But rather than rebuilding, they were restrained using stainless steel straps and ties.

down, saturating the masonry below and attracting salt damage. Where brick or stone is crumbling, it may be possible to open up the roof around this point, prop the stack and repair it in situ.

If you have a leaning stack, do not assume it will need rebuilding. Chimneys commonly lean and it may have been like this for hundreds of years. If you are in any doubt, a structural engineer with experience in old buildings should be consulted, but get a second opinion if you feel he is being overly cautious. A stainless steel strap and tie rod may be all that is required.

If the chimney condition is too perilous to repair in situ, it may require rebuilding. Take time to measure and

Top tip: Redundant stacks

If you are closing off a disused chimney stack, ensure that ventilation is provided to prevent condensation within the flue; an air brick inserted as high as possible on the least conspicuous side is generally recommended. Avoid dismantling stacks completely: they add interest to a roofline and their absence may spoil the appearance of your house.

Left: Repairing a chimney stack.
Top: This is a typical pattern of decay in a stack of soft brick incorporating no damp-proof course. Water saturates the stack and salts decay the masonry just below the roofline.
Centre: In order to repair this in situ, the roof is opened up to enable the damaged brickwork to be carefully cut away.
Bottom: New bricks are inserted and bedded in hydraulic lime mortar.

Below: In situ repair by a skilled craftsman means that the majority of the chimney has been retained intact.

photograph the stack before dismantling to enable accurate reinstatement. Remember, overhanging brick details are there for a reason – they protect the lower part of the stack by shedding water clear of the masonry below. Dismantling should be carried out with great care as many of the bricks or stones will be re-useable.

Terminating the top of your chimney stack

Chimney pots were not common until the eighteenth century, when fireplaces and flues were dramatically reduced in size to improve efficiency. The addition of the pot raised the height of the chimney, and hence improved the draw. Before this time, chimneys had large flues that were simply left open to the elements. Any rainwater that entered the flue was absorbed into the flue walls and evaporated out through the action of heat and draught.

As a general rule, leave your chimney termination as it was intended – the chances are that it will work as it always did. However, there are exceptions when an alteration may need to be made:

> If your fireplace suffers from downdraught.
> If you have had a stainless steel liner fitted that will otherwise channel rainwater down its non-absorbent sides, causing a puddle on your hearth or corrosion in your stove.
> If your chimney is attractive to nesting birds.
> If your flue is deteriorating due to saturation from rain entering at the top.

If you have chimney pots, a simple stainless steel rain hat with integral bird guard, powder-coated to match, may suffice. Purpose-made pots incorporating a cowl are available, but make sure you choose one that is suitable for your appliance. Most are designed for gas rather than solid fuel.

Right: A raincap of some description is essential if a metal liner has been installed. This cap has been powder-coated to match the buff-coloured pot.

Inglenooks and fireplaces in older houses are usually served by a chunky stack with no pots; here, a flagstone raised on stones or bricks may provide a more appropriate rain cap. Ensure that the opening at the sides is adequate to allow a draw, and make sure it is properly anchored and will not blow off in high winds. Also, be aware that this little roof to the flue creates a splendid environment for nesting jackdaws! Grilles may need to be incorporated to keep them out.

While a rain cap or cowl may solve certain chimney problems, it may also affect the draw, particularly of a large flue serving an inglenook. Always experiment by mocking up your preferred solution before striking the scaffold and committing yourself.

The Rumford revolution

Inefficient and smoking fireplaces were common until Benjamin Thompson, Count Rumford, developed a formula in the 1790s to calculate the optimum dimensions for the opening in relation to the flue. This work had a dramatic effect on the design of hob grates, resulting in many inglenooks being closed in to create smaller openings.

BURNING WITHOUT SMOKE

The principles seem very simple yet, in reality, getting a fire to burn efficiently without creating room smoke can be fraught with difficulty. Diagnosing the problem and then experimenting is the key to finding a solution.

> **Flue blockages** Nesting birds can very quickly deposit huge quantities of twigs in your flue during spring. Check for blockages by having your chimney swept and cleared.

> **Size of opening** The fireplace opening may be too large for the size of the flue, particularly if you have an inglenook. Close down the opening by fitting a canopy or raising the hearth. Experiment with opening sizes using a non-combustible board.

> **Lack of ventilation to the room** Test this by opening a door to see if it improves the draw. If this is the case, fix a vent: either through an external wall or ducted underfloor to a grille in the hearth.

> **Downdraught** This is caused by the close proximity of a tree, building, hill, etc. on the windward side,

Above: A raised flagstone provides a more attractive raincap but ensure it does not affect the draw. Light a test fire while the scaffold is still in position.

Metal register plate to stop draughts

Canopy which can be easily lifted off to allow easy access for sweeping flue

Fire basket raised on bricks

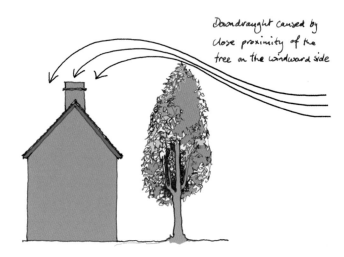

Downdraught caused by close proximity of the tree on the windward side

Left: A smoking inglenook can be improved in several ways. A canopy will assist in channelling smoke and reducing the effective opening size. This should be fitted in conjunction with a register plate to seal off the remaining flue opening. Ensure the canopy can be lifted off easily for regular sweeping. Raising the fire basket on bricks will also assist the draw.

Left below: Downdraught may be problematic on sites where large features such as trees and hills affect wind patterns.

diverting air currents and causing the draught to blow down the flue. Every situation is different, but it may be possible to reduce the height of a tree or, where a chimney stack has been lowered, restore it to its original height. Fitting a cowl or a raised slab is another approach, but this may have a detrimental effect on the draw.

The National Fireplace Association publishes useful guides that give advice on these problems.

Opening up a fireplace

Because of the inefficiency of inglenook fireplaces and their tendency to smoke, many have been reduced in size and fitted with Georgian, Victorian or even twentieth-century fire surrounds. There is often a temptation to take out the later addition and restore the inglenook to its original form. Be aware that, in taking such a step, you may be destroying a valuable or historically interesting feature which was much better at heating your room. You may also be disappointed at what you find (or do not find!) and have to embark on considerable work to make the structure safe.

Where fireplace openings have been altered or flues have fallen into disuse, special care needs to be taken in their reinstatement. They may have been altered or blocked up, and it is not unknown for new wooden joist ends to be sticking into redundant flues. Be sure that the flue will be safe and can be made to function effectively before embarking on major work.

Above: In this little Dorset cottage, the original inglenook has been periodically altered, the most recent addition being a 1950s surround which is probably vastly more efficient than the original arrangement. The temptation to 'restore' the inglenook may be great, but consider the consequences before you proceed.

THATCH AND CHIMNEYS

Fires in thatch are common, and owners of thatched houses should seek expert advice on minimising the risks. Consider the following points:

> It is particularly important that chimneys in thatched houses are maintained in good condition and do not leak.

> If there is a thick layer of thatch at the point where your stack penetrates the roof, it may be insulating the masonry and creating temperatures within your flue that are capable of causing spontaneous combustion. Consider inserting a fire barrier between the thatch and the masonry and a temperature sensor linked to an alarm system. This is vital if installing a multi-fuel stove.

> The chimney stack to a thatched roof should stand well above the ridge. If it does not, it may be necessary to raise the stack or reduce the thickness of the thatch when next recoating.

> Spark arrestors consist of a metal mesh fitted at the top of the stack. They are designed to prevent cinders escaping but, if they are not properly maintained and cleared, they actually increase the risk of fire.

> If you are having a liner fitted, go to a reputable firm and be sure to insulate it.

Above right: Chimneys and thatch can be a dangerous combination: the stack here is perilously close to the ridge. Be properly informed about the issues, maintain your chimney on a regular basis and check your insurance cover.

Chimney checklist

> Get your chimney swept regularly by an experienced sweep.

> Use binoculars once a year to check the condition of the stack.

> Check that wood for burning is dry and well seasoned; ash and oak are ideal.

> Check your roof space annually while the fire is lit for any signs of smoke leakage.

> If in doubt, get a specialist chimney surveyor with a camera to check the condition.

> In addition to normal alarms, fit a smoke alarm in your roof space and a carbon monoxide alarm in the living area.

> Never go to bed leaving a fire unguarded.

Above: Always use an experienced and careful chimney sweep.

Windows, doors and joinery

Whether they have a lopsided squint or an assured symmetry, doors and windows form the faces and define the character of our homes. The quality of the joinery says much about the status of a house and its original owners, and is a good tool for dating a building.

The term joinery refers to the visible finished woodwork in a house, including panelling, doors, doorcases, skirtings, dado rails, cornices, shutters, shutter boxes, windows, window frames and staircases. Where such features remain they add value and character but, sadly, woodwork is often needlessly and inappropriately replaced.

Until the middle of the nineteenth century, joiners used only hand tools so there were minute irregularities in the items produced, making each unique. All joinery should be regarded in the same way as antique furniture: you would not discard a 200-year-old table just because it had a damaged leg!

Well-maintained joinery can last for many centuries and, where necessary, should be repaired in situ by a skilled joiner. Generally repair is a far less expensive option than installing an entirely new item. If this is unavoidable, any new work should be done on a like-for-like basis using matching materials, traditional construction techniques and well-seasoned timber. It is worth remembering that a great deal of the softwood used in old joinery was far more durable that its modern equivalent; this is a good reason in itself for retaining as much as possible during repair.

Opposite: Although rather marred by the 'modernised' upper window, the character of this house in County Tyrone, Northern Ireland, is defined by the external joinery.

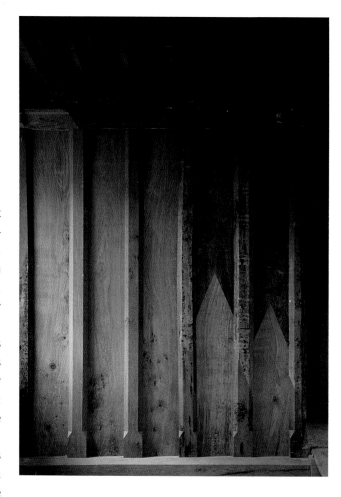

Above: Repairs to this cross-passage plank and muntin partition have been carefully executed to ensure as much of the original fabric as possible is retained.

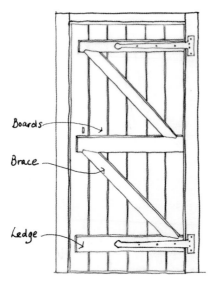

Ⓐ Simple boarded, ledged and braced door

Boards

Brace

Ledge

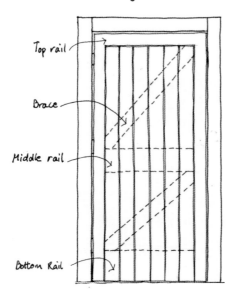

Ⓑ Framed, ledged and braced door

Top rail

Brace

Middle rail

Bottom Rail

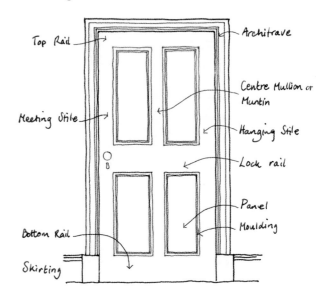

Ⓒ Panelled Door

Top Rail

Meeting Stile

Bottom Rail

Skirting

Architrave

Centre Mullion or Muntin

Hanging Stile

Lock rail

Panel

Moulding

DOORS

Doors developed from a simple construction of vertical planks fixed to horizontal timber 'ledges', and evolved into complicated joinery items with panels and frames. Key points to remember when maintaining your door:

> External doors are most likely to have deteriorated along their bottom edge due to damp. New timber can usually be scarfed in to replace the rotten part. 4

> Due to their large area, external doors may shrink and swell several millimetres with the seasons, so think twice before trimming the edges during damp weather.

> Thorough decoration can minimise shrinkage and swelling. Always take a door off its hinges so that all the edges can be properly primed and finished; this must include all bare timber such as within the letter plate opening.

> If you are changing your floor covering, the bottom of a door may need trimming. Always think twice before making irreversible changes, particularly as the floor covering may be only temporary.

> Many problems with doors are related to their hinges. It is always worth checking that they are working properly and not worn, loose or binding.

Above: basic door types.

A: A simple boarded, ledged and braced door, typically used in cottage interiors. Note the direction of the braces pointing downwards towards the hinge.

B: A framed, ledged and braced door, more suitable for exterior use since the frame resists the buckling of the door when it gets wet.

C: A framed and panelled door; the configuration and profile of the panels are usually a good indicator of the date.

Left: The lower part of this door and its frame had been damaged by rot. Rather than replace it in its entirety, new wood has been inserted, retaining and adding to its history. Once the door is painted, the repair will be all but invisible.

Left: Frequently it is only the very bottom of a frame or doorcase that is rotten. Here, a joiner is cutting out the damaged wood ready for patch repairs.

Top tip: Retaining value

Often it is believed that replacing windows and doors increases the value of your house. In the case of an old building, the exact opposite is frequently true: many potential buyers are put off by such changes. Original features are much sought after, and inappropriate replacement may spoil the character not only of an individual building but an entire street.

Above: The windows and doors added to the facade of this Isle of Wight cottage may be an attempt to make it seem quaint. In reality, they bear little relationship to any historic precedent and merely disturb the building's proportions and character.

Above: Items such as doors are best repaired on the bench, where it is much easier to check all the joints and make good any defects.

Although it is important to ensure a good fit in the frame, painting the door before it is re-hung will enable all surfaces, including the top and bottom edges, to be fully coated. This reduces the chance of moisture absorption which can cause doors to swell and stick.

Above: Fanlights were often part of an elaborate doorcase, as in this six-panel door in West Sussex, typical of the Georgian period.

Maintenance of all the elements is vital to ensure that rot does not take hold. Great care should be taken to preserve original glass.

Fanlights

Glazed fanlights began to appear in the 1720s to provide natural light for the hallway. These were nearly always separate from the door itself (unlike the corrupted 'Georgian-style' doors sold today with 'slipped' fanlights). Wood, iron, lead, brass and cast iron were all used in their construction at various times. Because of their intricate nature, considerable care should be taken in their repair.

Fire regulations

Many internal doors are replaced or damaged because of the need to comply with fire regulations, particularly where loft conversions are undertaken. It may be possible to adapt and upgrade original doors to meet these requirements, using fire-resisting materials and intumescent products. If intumescent seals are used, they are best fitted to the door lining rather than the door itself. If all else fails, the integrity of the door can be retained by fitting fire-retardant board to just one side, making it flush. It is not necessarily an attractive solution, but it is reversible.

Top tip: Draughts and noise

Brush strips along the bottom edge of external doors help cut draughts. Movable draught excluders made of fabric and filled with sand are an effective and less intrusive alternative.

Letter plates can let in cold air, and may need their springs replaced to ensure that they close properly. A wooden flap or heavy piece of cloth fitted to the inside face of the letter plate will provide added insulation. Escutcheons with cover plates are a good way of cutting draughts from keyholes.

Right: An escutcheon protects the woodwork from damage as a key is inserted. A cover plate stops draughts; this should hang loosely enough to fall always into position over the keyhole.

WINDOWS

Some windows are made of metal – wrought iron, cast iron, steel or aluminium – but the great majority are wood. The two basic opening types are hinged casements and sliding sashes. Those that do not open are known as fixed lights. Timber windows have a very long life if well maintained. The proportions, detailing and glazing pattern of original windows are fundamental to the integrity of a building's facade. Replacement should be considered only if absolutely necessary.

Top: Casement windows are the opposite of sashes, hinged rather than sliding. This eighteenth-century wrought iron casement hangs on 'pintle' hinges within a wooden frame; the 'pentice' roof protects the window from rain and the hook or 'stay' holds it open.

Above: The fact that this timber casement is designed for larger panes dates it to after the middle of the nineteenth century and the advent of drawn sheet glass. Note the stone sill that sheds water clear of the wall.

Assessing window condition

Inspect each window in your home in turn to see what problems there might be.

> Make a plan of the house and give each window a number, then list the specific repairs required.
> Use a penknife to check for rotten wood (sound timber resists penetration) or, in the case of metal windows, rust. Pay particular attention

Left: This seventeenth-century timber frame has been altered to insert a large nineteenth-century window. As a result, the wall is bulging and the window may have to be taken out to facilitate structural repairs. This would be a good opportunity to overhaul the window as well, while retaining as much original glass as possible.

to the sill and lower parts of the frame as these are most vulnerable.

> Note all loose joints.
> If necessary, strip paint away to gain a clearer idea of the window's condition.
> Note any broken panes. If they are handmade, can they be left in situ?
> Check for loose, cracked or damaged putty.
> From the inside, feel for draughts. A general overhaul is a good time to address this problem.
> Check sash cords and hinges.
> Ensure that sashes slide freely and are perfectly counterbalanced by the weights.
> Open weight pockets to check for obstructions. A musty smell indicates dampness and possible decay.
> Make sure window furniture functions correctly.
> If removing more than one window, ensure that each is labelled and a note is made of its position in the building.

Left: A complete rail of this sash window has been replaced while the base of one stile has been scarfed in. Any good joiner should be able to make such a repairs.

Below left: Simple repairs to timber windows use metal brackets. The small crack in the glass is minor enough not to necessitate sacrificing the entire pane.

Below: Repairing a rotten sill by inserting good-quality new timber is a relatively easy job for a joiner. Water must be prevented from running down into the junction between the new sill and the old frame.

Below right: Paint-sealed windows can be released with care and a little patience. Support might be needed in case the paint is the only thing holding the sash in place.

Repairs

The simplest form of repair is the strengthening of the corner of a rotten wooden window with a metal angle bracket. New sections to rails, stiles, glazing bars and frames can be scarfed in by a good joiner. In all such repairs, the minimum amount of existing timber should be removed to allow an effective repair to be formed.

Often windows have loose joints which may simply be re-glued. Bear in mind that the frame may not be square so, rather than cramping it together on a work-

Resin repairs

The use of fillers and two-part resin systems to repair external woodwork sometimes exacerbates problems of rot because moisture becomes trapped. Despite this, resin may be a sensible option where removal of an item of joinery for repairs, perhaps in the case of a window or door frame, would cause significant damage to the fabric of the building or where complete replacement of the item would otherwise be necessary. The system employed must be flexible, and the work undertaken only by those trained in the use of the products and techniques required for the preparation of the timber.

Left: Original sash windows add to a sense of proportion and cohesion in this Victorian London terrace.

Below: While it is usually easier to remove a sash for major work, simple repairs can be undertaken while the window is in situ.

bench, place it in the actual frame and use small wedges of wood to keep the joints tight until the glue is dry.

Sills may often be repaired by cutting the rotten face back to sound wood and then planting on a new piece, using glue and non-ferrous screws to fix it. Do use good-quality handpicked timber and ensure that there is a drip groove along the underside of the sill.

To open a window which has been painted shut, try running a blade carefully around the edges. However, windows might have been screwed or nailed shut; if they fail to move relatively easily, ascertain whether this is the case rather than try to force them open.

Sash windows

Sashes generally are vertical-sliding, suspended on cords and counterbalanced by lead or cast iron weights contained in the box frame of the window. There is a simpler form, the 'Yorkshire' sash, in which the sashes slide horizontally without the benefit of weights.

Sash windows are often a mystery to the homeowner, yet they are straightforward to overhaul and can almost always be repaired. For anything other than minor repairs, it is usually best to remove them from their frames. This is relatively simple and is done from inside.

Sticking sashes can have a variety of causes, such as over-painting, swollen or distorted frames, distortion to the beads that hold the sashes in place, loose joints on the sashes or seized pulleys. Pulleys should be freed and oiled; tallow or beeswax applied to the edges of sashes may help make them run more smoothly.

Always try to retain old glass. If it has to be replaced, it must be of the same thickness and weight as the original for the sash to be correctly balanced by its weights. If a sash cord is broken, always repair the cords on both sides. Sash cords come in a range of thicknesses; ensure that new cord is strong enough for the weight of the window.

A number of companies specialise in repairing and draughtproofing sash windows, fully overhauling them and, if necessary, making new ones.

Right: Re-cording a sash window can usually be carried out from the inside. A helper is useful to support the sashes.

A. Remove the 'staff beads' with a chisel. These are usually pinned in place and can be re-used. Free the inner sash: cut the cords, leaving them as long as possible, and gently lower the weights into the pockets so the sash can be removed.

B. Remove the 'parting bead' which separates the two sashes; this is not fixed, but wedged into a groove in the frame so should be easy to release. Remove the outer sash in the same way as the inner sash.

C. Take out the 'pocket piece' with a thin screwdriver to minimise damage; it should not be glued or nailed but simply wedged into position. Then remove the weights.

D. Tie a nail or screw to a length of string and thread it over the outer pulley. Measure the total length of the old cord and cut the new cord accordingly. Attach the cord to the string and pull the cord through and down into the pocket.

E. Attach the cord to the weight. Pull the weight back up inside the box and attach the end of the cord to the outer sash with screws so that it can easily be adjusted. Fit the second cord and then check that the window runs up and down. Reassemble the window elements, re-cording the inner sash in the process.

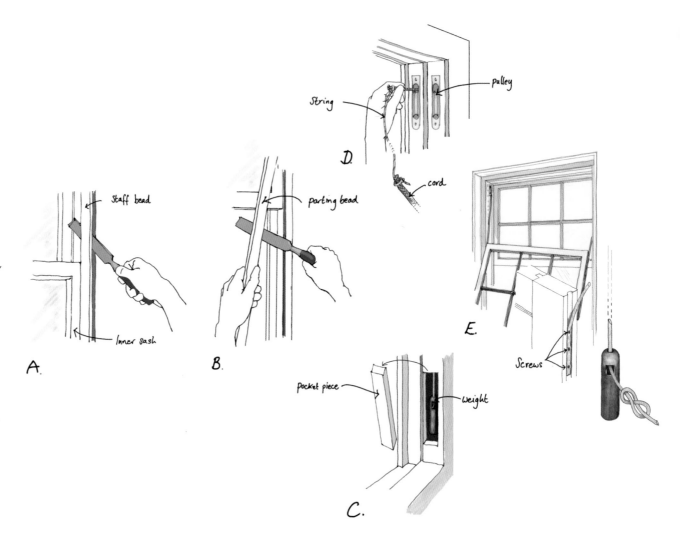

Top tip: Redecorating a sash window

When sashes are removed from their frames, they are easy to redecorate. You will need to rub them down carefully and prepare the surface first. Choose a good-quality paint system of primer, undercoat and topcoat. If you are taking them back to bare wood, linseed oil paint is likely to provide the greatest longevity. Use a 'sash brush' with a pointed end to get into the corners.

Reducing noise and heat loss

It is not usually possible to replace old window glass with a double-glazed unit since the rebates in both sashes and casements are not deep enough. While it may be tempting to replace your entire window with a double-glazed version, the benefits that this brings will never outweigh the profound aesthetic impact on the building. Instead, there are a variety of low-impact choices:

> Rattling windows may be wedged; with sash windows, a fastener with a cam action can be fitted, which draws the two sashes together.

> Shutters and heavy curtains reduce draughts and keep heat in.

> Most heat is lost through cracks around the frame. Many companies specialise in draughtproofing sash windows, installing inconspicuous 'brush' strips to the top edge, meeting rails and parting beads which

Left: To fit draughtproofing 'brushes', grooves are routed in the edge of the sashes.

Below left: Brush strips are fitted into the grooves and will be virtually hidden once the sash is replaced in the frame.

Left: Specialist companies fit inconspicuous lift-out secondary glazing panels, which are held in place by magnetic strips. These panels can be lifted out and stored during the summer months.

Right: Metal windows with leaded panes such as these in Suffolk have simplicity and elegance when they are properly maintained.

also helps reduce noise. Avoid the use of plastic staff beads and parting beads.

> Secondary glazing is now far less visually intrusive than it used to be, and can be powder-coated to match your paintwork. Lift-out magnetic panels are ideal for reducing heat loss during winter. Sliding secondary glazing allows windows to be opened, but is more visible.

Metal windows

Early metal windows were of wrought iron glazed with leaded lights. From the mid-eighteenth century, cast iron was used. Steel windows started to appear in the second half of the nineteenth century; with Crittall the main manufacturer, that name became somewhat generic.

Common problems with metal windows include rust, distortion, excessive paint build-up and failed hinges and fittings. But even windows that seem to be well beyond repair may be overhauled.

> Unprotected metal windows will quickly accumulate rust on the surface, so always apply a priming coat as soon as practicable.

> Where rust is present purely on the surface, it can simply be cleaned off using wire brushes.

> Long-term protection can be provided for steel windows by hot-dip galvanising; this may result in severe damage to old windows so always take advice first.

> Damaged or corroded parts of steel or wrought iron windows can be cut out and a replacement section welded in. With steel windows, specialist steel window companies work either on site or in the workshop. Your local blacksmith can probably carry out repairs to wrought iron windows.

> Repairs to cast iron are likely to require a process known as cold-metal stitching.
> Draughtproofing may be provided using a system where the opening edge of the casement is temporarily coated with a release agent. A silicone sealant is then injected into the gap between the closed window and its frame. When the sealant has dried to fill the air gap, the window is opened and the release agent cleaned away.

Leaded lights

Although they are valued for their aesthetics, leaded lights were created for purely practical reasons: glass was once available only in small panes. By using thin 'H'-shaped strips of lead, 'cames', to hold the small, often diamond-shaped panes of clear or coloured glass known as 'quarries', it was possible to create larger glazed panels. The cames were soldered at the joints and the gaps between the lead and glass were packed with special 'cement'.

Once assembled, leaded lights were fitted either into framed windows or directly into masonry openings. Panels of leaded glass sag if unsupported, so metal 'saddlebars' or 'ferramenta' were fitted across the opening. The leaded window was then attached to these, using copper wires soldered to the lead.

Above: Leaded lights incorporating coloured glass are common in Victorian and Edwardian houses. This example has been carefully repaired and cleaned.

Above: Despite its collapse, there is still sufficient evidence of the design of this leaded light for it to be reinstated.

Above: Unusually, wood provides the support for this leaded window. The lead strip has been soldered to the wooden panels and twisted to hold it in place.

One of the most frequent problems with leaded light panels is that they buckle or bulge because of deterioration of the leading; this in turn causes the glass to crack and water to seep through. Some panels will need only careful flattening, localised soldering and cleaning; others will require a complete rebuild. If a leaded light is to be dismantled, a useful way of making an exact record of it is to take a 'rubbing'. Luckily there are many specialist firms able to undertake repairs.

With coloured or stained glass windows, damaged pieces are sometimes mended with special adhesive and placed between layers of plain glass before the window is re-leaded. Original stained glass windows should be regarded as highly as works of art: their repair and conservation should be entrusted to experts.

GLASS

Unlike the smooth and regular look of modern glass, old glass was handmade and contained irregularities, bubbles and waves. Rather than detracting from its appearance, they give it life so that it flashes and sparkles as it reflects the light. If your old windows contain original glass, treat it with special care and retain it wherever possible. Always think twice before replacing a handmade pane that has suffered minor damage, for instance a small crack across the corner. Try to save the glass even if the window itself is beyond repair.

Glazing repairs

Often the glass pane is intact but the putty is cracked, loose or missing and letting in water. Ideally, cracked putty should be removed and replaced, but this is almost impossible to achieve without breaking the pane.

> If the window is in a relatively sheltered location, it may be possible to fill the cracks in the old putty by warming up some new linseed oil putty and rubbing it in with your finger.

> Where sections of putty are loose, gently remove them and re-putty the gaps.

Above: The beauty of old glass is clear to see in the small panes of this leaded window. Unlike modern glass, it is uneven and contains imperfections that help it to throw out varied reflections.

Right: A specialist 'putty lamp' uses focused infrared heat to soften the putty above and beneath the glass prior to removal. Infrared rays pass through glass without heating it, so the pane is not damaged.

> On an exposed elevation, cracked putty will need to be replaced to stop the window from leaking. Where the glass is fine, consider taking the window to a specialist joiner who has a 'putty lamp' – this will soften the putty without damaging the glass.

> Never use a heat gun to soften old putty: it will almost certainly crack the glass.

Re-glazing

> Always clean up and prime the rebate before puttying in the new pane to prevent the oils from the putty being absorbed and drying out too quickly.

> Use fixing pins, 'sprigs', on larger panes but ensure that you leave a small gap between them and the glass to prevent fracturing.

> Use a putty knife and linseed oil putty.

> Leave putty for at least a week in a warmish environment before painting it.

> Never underestimate the skill involved in creating a neat finish with putty!

Types of glass

Cylinder, muff or broad glass Made by blowing a long cylinder of glass which was then split lengthways and flattened. This glass is characterised by straight ripples and by occasional 'seeds' or bubbles.

Crown glass This was of much higher quality than cylinder glass, and predominated in the Georgian period. Molten glass was blown into a balloon shape, a 'punty' rod was attached and the glass was then spun rapidly until a disc was formed, causing characteristic circular lines. The outer portion was cut into small panes while the central portion, marred by a knob left by the punty, was traditionally used for less important windows. True crown glass is no longer made.

Right: The distinctive spun pattern of crown glass can clearly be seen here, projected on to the wall as the sunlight passes through the window. Such beautiful glass is easily lost when repairing windows if great care is not taken.

Drawn sheet glass Invented in the 1830s, it was a cheap method for producing large sheets of glass. It changed window fashions dramatically: multi-paned sashes and casements utilising smaller panes virtually disappeared.
Modern glass Machine-drawn cylinder glass was introduced in the early twentieth century, followed by flat-drawn sheet glass. In 1959, the invention of float glass revolutionised the manufacturing process because of its high quality and cheaper production costs.

SHUTTERS

Before the introduction of window glass, shutters were vital. Evidence for internal and external shutters can often be found on earlier buildings.

Left: The use of larger, heavier sheets of glass led to the introduction of 'horns' on sash windows, to give added strength to the meeting rail junction.

Below left: External shutters were never as popular in Britain as in the rest of Europe. The broad glazing bars of this window in Somerset indicate an early eighteenth-century origin but it may well have replaced an earlier window.

Below right: The frame to this early panelling uses 'mason's mitres', rather than true 45-degree mitres. The scribe-marks for setting out are still visible on the rail.

From the Georgian period onwards, internal shutters were generally folded back into reveals at the sides of the window. Since they were originally designed to be unobtrusive, it is sometimes not immediately evident that shutters exist: they may have become hidden by layers of paint or have been screwed back into the reveals. Careful exploration is always worthwhile.

Working shutters are a great way of keeping in heat and deterring burglars, so it is worth spending time making them operational or considering reinstating them where they are missing. A blacksmith can make new stay bars, but avoid modern brass catches, which look inappropriate on heavy Georgian shutters.

PANELLING

Panelling, sometimes known as wainscoting, has three key horizontal elements: a skirting board at the foot of the wall, a dado or chair rail about a metre up, and a cornice at the top.

At first oak was used but this was superseded by cheaper softwoods. From 1720, full-height panelling began to go out of fashion, although many rooms were still panelled to dado height since it helped to protect against damp. The various elements were fixed together with simple joints, wooden pegs, glue and nails. The panels themselves were formed of planks butt-jointed together. These were not fixed in any way but sat in thin

grooves cut in the framing, allowing them to contract and expand.

Where panelling has been in contact with a damp floor or wall, it may have suffered localised rot and require repair. It might be possible to repair the rotten sections without disturbing the rest. Dismantling should be avoided where possible. When it is undertaken, a detailed photographic record and numbering of the pieces prior to removal are strongly advised.

IRONMONGERY

Individual items of ironmongery, and the screws with which they are fixed, provide useful clues for dating joinery. Where replacement is unavoidable, for instance if hinges are too worn to function properly, it is worth labelling and preserving the original.

Early ironmongery was hand-forged in wrought iron by local blacksmiths. In Georgian times, door furniture was mass-produced in cast iron, with polished brass reserved for the wealthy. Letter plates first appeared on doors with the introduction of the penny post in 1840; to accommodate them, new doors had a wider lock rail.

Left: Wrought iron, as opposed to cast iron, has a beaten quality, as in this hinge which sits on a 'pintle' driven into the wall.

Below left: Letter plates come in a range of shapes and sizes and should be selected to suit the style of door. Take care with earlier doors, which may lack a wide enough lock rail.

Right: Old locks, such as this one from around 1840, are an important part of the history of a house, so should be retained in situ wherever possible, even if they no longer serve their intended function.

Often, ironmongery has been painted over and the detail lost. Chemical paint removers may be used to reveal the metal, but beware of using sharp tools which may scratch the surface. In some cases, a blacksmith may be able to undertake repairs to damaged items.

Hinges

If a hinge fails or wears, the door will drop, resulting in the door sticking or the lock being affected. Choice of the right hinge depends on the type of door, its material, and its weight and use. Style is another consideration – for example, a 'T' hinge is best for medieval doors and 'H' or 'HL' hinges for Georgian panel doors. These are now readily available from specialist suppliers.

Where nails are used to fix traditional hinges, they must be hammered right through to the reverse side of the door then bent over to stop them pulling out. When fixing hinges to the frame, it is best to use screws as this allows adjustments to be made.

Steel hinges should be wiped over with an oily rag to prevent rust, with the moving parts either lightly oiled or, if the door is subjected to a lot of traffic, greased. If hinges are being fixed against green oak, they are best painted on the back to prevent the steel from staining the wood. A rust inhibitor is advisable as a pre-treatment to painting.

Locks

There are two basic types of lock: a rim lock, which is fitted to the face or rim of the door, and a mortise lock, which is set within the thickness of the door. When an old lock becomes difficult to use it should be repaired by an expert; if it is likely to be damaged by removal, always call in a locksmith.

Left: A locking security bolt is easy to fit and relatively inconspicuous; it allows sashes to be secure even when ajar.

Below: The parts of a staircase. 'Closed string' stairs (A) developed from the seventeenth century into complex 'cut string' stairs from the eighteenth century through to the Edwardian period (B). The pitch of the stair is determined by the 'rise' and the 'going' (C).

STAIRCASES

In its simplest form, a staircase may consist of treads and risers fixed to bearers and constructed in situ. A higher-quality staircase would be constructed in a workshop as a complete unit, using diagonal boards, 'strings', into which the treads and risers were rebated. Newel posts top and bottom provided fixing points for handrails and strengthened the treads where they turned a corner.

Repairs

Creaking treads are just one of the problems that can beset a wooden staircase; others are rot, beetle infestation or simple wear. Repairs are easiest where there is access both from above and below, but do not cause unnecessary damage to achieve this.

Use screws to tighten treads and risers from above to stop them creaking. Where access from underneath is possible, check the blocks that hold them together and replace or re-glue them if necessary. If the joints between your stairs and string have become loose, new wedges should be glued and driven into the joint from below.

Keys are as important as the lock itself. Have a duplicate cut so there is always a spare. If a key is missing, a good locksmith should be able to make a new one.

Locks need to be kept clean. Avoid dipping them to remove paint and dirt, since this can damage the mechanism. Use good-quality lock oil or graphite-based oil or grease, always sparingly: too much will make the inside of the lock sticky and attract dirt, which can damage the mechanism. Where metal is gilded or lacquered, be careful not to over-clean. A card or metal template, cut to fit around the lock, will prevent cleaning materials from damaging the woodwork.

Be aware of the requirements of insurance companies, since original locks rarely offer the level of security required today. Modern mortise locks can be fitted into the edge of the door so that they are virtually hidden. Where an existing lock is being replaced, take it with you when you buy the new one, or measure or trace its exact position and dimensions, to avoid needing to cut new and unnecessary holes.

Small mortise security bolts provide an inconspicuous way of protecting casement windows, while special bolts can be fitted into holes drilled in sashes. Alternatively, a locking bolt allows sashes to be secure even while ajar.

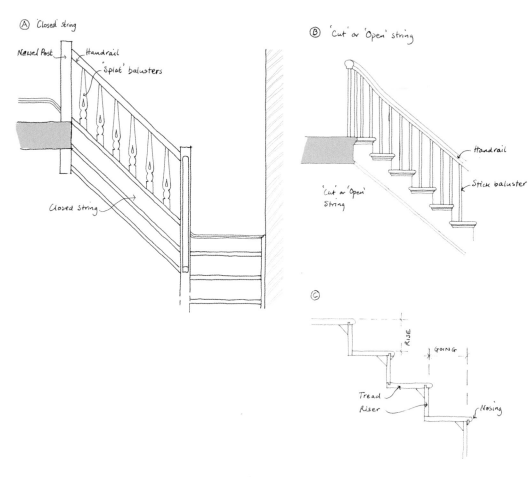

Left: In the past, staircases did not have to comply with building regulations; it is not unusual to find odd arrangements in old buildings.

Above left: A simple closed string stair, with stick balusters and an elegant, turned newel post.

Left: A good joiner should be able to repair a staircase; where treads are unsafe they may have to be replaced. The bearers under the treads are made from hardwood for added durability.

Staircase rules and regulations

New staircases require building regulation approval. To meet these requirements, modern staircases are much more regular in their appearance than traditional ones. Importantly, they have to meet certain criteria in terms of their steepness, the rise and the going, the headroom, the handrails and the balusters. As a result, it is not always possible to slot a new staircase into an available space in an old building.

With staircases there is always a balance between safety and conservation. If, for example, treads are badly worn they may have to be replaced. Even so, if only the nosings are damaged, the front edge of the tread can be cut off and replaced with a new length of suitably shaped timber screwed and glued into place.

Split or broken spindles are a frequent problem. Often it is possible to glue and temporarily splint them. The other option is to reinforce a broken spindle by using a dowel drilled into the end of each piece.

MOULDINGS

In early buildings, the structural timbers themselves were often moulded to provide decoration. The Georgian era saw the use of applied timber mouldings, such as architraves, which were fashioned by hand using a range of moulding planes. In mid-Victorian times, machinery revolutionised manufacture.

Always retain original mouldings. When carrying out work such as erecting stud walls, do not cut through mouldings but instead shape the new work around them; the mouldings will still be intact if the new work is ever removed.

The nails used to fix mouldings were usually driven either directly into the masonry or into wooden plugs or battens. Be careful if temporarily removing them since they are easily split.

11

Plasters, renders and roughcast

It is commonly believed that, when you are 'renovating' an old building, the first job is to strip all the plaster from the interior. Yet, in nearly all cases, this approach is unnecessary and misguided. Old plasters and renders give a building texture, character and beauty and are straightforward to repair.

Traditional lime plaster lets walls breathe and absorbs excess humidity. It is warmer to the touch and therefore condensation is reduced. Most important of all, it looks right for an old house. Texture and finish are ultimately the things that differentiate between a heavy-handed renovation and a carefully considered repair which will sustain the value of your home in the longer term. Externally, lime render and roughcast provide the ideal breathable coating for a solid walled structure; finished with limewash, this has an aesthetic which is a million miles away from modern cement and plastic paint.

Unfortunately, the fashion for stripping plasters and renders continues, exposing interior and exterior stone and brick walls. This look is not traditional: random rubble masonry would never have been left exposed, inside or out, even in the humblest of dwellings. Ceilings have suffered a similar fate, often being removed to show off the structure of the floor above; historically, only joists with chamfers and chamfer stops would have been exposed in this way.

It is important to understand the process of plastering, especially when commissioning work. It is a highly skilled job, and an amateur would struggle to achieve anything like an acceptable finish.

Opposite: External roughcasting has for several decades been associated with the grey and flat cements that we have grown to hate. This recently reinstated lime roughcast in Gloucestershire is something quite different: the hand-thrown finish clings to the undulations of the stonework and glows as the naturally pigmented limewash reflects the light.

Right: An example of how beautiful a lime finish can be. The original roughcast to these two cottages has been patch-repaired and decorated with limewash tinted in natural earth pigments. The quoins 'separating' the two buildings have also been made up in smooth lime render and coloured to give the appearance of stone.

Left: The left-hand house shows the traditional lime roughcast finish, originally limewashed to protect the underlying layers. The right-hand house has fallen victim to the cult of 'rubble worship': it has been stripped of its finish and repointed in cement.

INTERNAL PLASTERWORK

If you are lucky enough to have historic plaster in your home, cherish it. In recent decades, old houses have frequently been re-plastered using a modern gypsum plaster, or even in a hard sand and cement finish, in a misguided attempt to hold back damp. Historic ceilings are all too frequently discarded and replaced with plasterboard; this is tragic when they could so easily have been repaired and character retained.

Up until World War II, your house would probably have been plastered in a lime-based material, mixed with animal hair to reduce shrinkage. Ceilings were made by fixing laths on to the joists, with gaps between to squeeze the plaster through to form a key. Studwork partitions were formed in a similar way. Most laths were 'riven' – split along the grain – in Baltic fir, chestnut or oak, often right up to the 1950s. Sawn softwood started to emerge around the mid-nineteenth century as a cheaper, though less durable, alternative.

Water reed is commonly found as a substrate where it was readily available, especially in vernacular buildings. In damper climates, particularly in high-quality Georgian and Victorian houses, external walls were sometimes 'dry lined' by fixing timber studs to the interior face and plastering on to the laths rather than directly on to the masonry.

Top tip: was it once plastered?

The fashion for stripping plasters has resulted in many houses losing their historic authenticity.

> Externally, look for window surrounds that stand proud of the face of the building. This may indicate an earlier coat of render which has been removed. Traces of the original finish can often be found behind gutters and fascia boards.

> Internally, masonry was always plastered. The fashion for 'feature walls' of exposed stone is historically ridiculous. If you are uncertain about whether your exposed joists were once covered with a plaster ceiling, simply look for evidence of nail holes where the original laths would have been fixed.

Above: Externally, most rubble stone would have been finished in some way. This building in Gloucestershire would certainly have been rendered with lime, unifying the various additions to give it a polite and symmetrical facade. The window surrounds provide further evidence, set proud of the walls to allow for the thickness of the render.

Below: The fashion for internal 'feature walls' of exposed stone persists, yet it bears no resemblance to the original interior. This example is also confused by exposed joists: these would have been concealed under a lime plaster ceiling.

Left: Water reed was often used as an alternative to lath as a base of plaster. There would have been an abundance of the material near this house in Somerset.

Plaster for flat work on walls and ceilings in traditional buildings would have been based on lime or clay, or a combination of both, mixed with sand. A binder was added to give it strength and reduce shrinkage, usually goat or cattle hair, although hay was sometimes used. Plaster was applied in one, two or three coats depending on the quality of the building.

When applied to lath, the first coat is described as a 'pricking up coat'. This refers to the way the plaster 'pricks' through the gaps between the laths. The first coat on masonry is called a 'rendering coat' and is designed to bring it up to a reasonably flat surface. Both of these were 'scratched' in a diamond pattern to create a good key, and both can also be referred to as 'scratch' coats.

Choosing your plasterer

The use of lime plasters, renders and roughcasts requires skill and experience. While most plasterers can adapt to using lime with a few days' training, there is a great deal of risk attached to attempting lime work without a reasonable understanding of the material. Be vigilant for plasterers who think a lime render is basically a cement render with a bit of lime in it! Also be cautious about using plasterers inexperienced in lime who underestimate the extra skill required to produce a stable, crack-free finish.

> Ask your plasterer what mix he or she intends to use. Even the smallest amount of cement is unacceptable and negates the whole purpose of using lime.
> Ask how many coats will be applied – you will almost always need more than one.
> Ask how the substrate (the surface on to which the plaster is to be applied) will be prepared. If the lime plaster is going to work, it needs to go on to a porous or keyed substrate, wetted down in advance to control the suction.
> Ask how long it will be left between coats. This should be a minimum of a week, depending on how thick the coats are.

Above: Applying a lime plaster 'pricking up coat' to riven lath.

Left: Scratching the first coat to create a key, using a blunt-ended tool made from laths.

Above: A plasterer skilled in the use of lime may be difficult to find, but never compromise: better to wait and get the right one.

For good-quality work where a flat and level surface was required, and particularly in houses from the mid-1600s onwards, an intermediate coat, called a 'floating coat' or a 'straightening coat', was applied. This was carefully worked and levelled to get the coat dead flat using a 'floating rule', a perfectly straight length of timber which was passed across the ceiling or wall to check for bumps and hollows. The surface of the floating coat was then scratched using a 'devil float' which had nails pricked through it; this was applied to the surface using a light circular motion to provide a key for the final coat.

The final coat, referred to as a 'setting coat' or 'skimming coat', provided a smooth surface. It was a mixture of lime putty and fine sand, just 2–3mm thick.

Decorative plasterwork

Plaster mouldings reflect distinct period styles. If you are replacing them, always be careful to select those that are appropriate in detail and size: a labourer's cottage will have far simpler ornamentation than a Georgian town house.

From the seventeenth century right up to World War II, some houses would have been finished with cornicing, run in situ. This was achieved by using a template and running it around the top of the wall over wet plaster to create the profile of the cornice.

By the mid-nineteenth century, mass production made available a huge variety of plaster details which could be ordered ready-formed from a catalogue and fixed in position on site. These items were known as 'fibrous plasterwork' as they incorporated a hessian scrim that strengthened the back. They included lengths of cornice purchased by the yard and ceiling roses,

Above left: Applying the floating coat over the scratched surface of the first coat.

Above: The floating coat is 'devilled' with a lighter scratch to receive the final coat.

corbels and other items formed in flexible gelatine moulds.

The repair of decorative plasterwork requires a high level of skill but specialist plasterers are still to be found. Provided part of the original cornice remains, missing sections can be made up by taking a mould from the existing and casting new pieces. Fibrous plasterwork details are available from specialist manufacturers but great care should be taken to ensure that items are appropriate to the scale, period and status of your home. Many off-the-peg mouldings are historically incorrect, so choose carefully. Often plasterwork detail is obscured under a build-up of paint layers; stripping these back should be undertaken with great caution (➠ Removing coatings, page 166).

If you have a fine decorative ceiling which has come away from the structure above, there are methods of reattaching it using glass-fibre gauzes and non-ferrous wire mesh. Such techniques need to be executed with great skill and are never a job for the amateur.

Above right: Forming cornice work in situ. The basic shape is 'cored out' with a rough lime and sand mix. Once dry, a finer mix is applied gauged with plaster of Paris.

Right: The final profile is created by running a template or 'running mould' along the length of the cornice.

*Above: Fine quality
seventeenth-century
plasterwork. Conservators
should always be employed
when repairing or stabilising
such special work.*

Above: Never destroy a lath and plaster ceiling just because it has a few cracks and bulges: it may be perfectly sound and simply repairable for a fraction of the cost of replacement. Here, however, the laths were so decayed that they could no longer support the weight of the plaster.

Above right: This ceiling was seriously dipping and from below looked alarming. Investigation of the condition of the 'ash pole' joists in the attic space above revealed that all that was required was a little extra support mid-span. A timber beam was installed above, and steel straps threaded under each ash pole and fixed back to the beam. This non-invasive repair retained the deflection in the ceiling but prevented it from getting any worse.

Assessing the condition of your ceiling

An old ceiling will often bulge and deflect and, in so doing, crack and split. But do not assume it needs to be replaced just because the surface is no longer flat and a few cracks have opened up. Traditional haired plasters can withstand a great deal of deflection and still retain their strength and, like so many surfaces in an old building, become more beautiful for these imperfections.

It is important, and relatively simple, to assess the condition of a ceiling to be sure it is not going to collapse. A badly cracked ceiling could be due to a weak floor structure. A good way to assess the problem is to ask someone to walk around on the floor above while you observe the ceiling below. Any excessive movement in the ceiling may indicate that the floor joists need strengthening. It is also worth checking that the plaster is still well adhered to the substrate. Prod it to make sure that it is well fixed and not likely to drop. You may be surprised at just how secure your historic ceiling is, despite evidence of cracking and movement.

If a ceiling is permanently deflected and 'dipping' in the middle it is important to understand why, so it may be necessary to examine the problem from above. This will involve either carefully lifting the floorboards in the room overhead, or crawling around an attic space.

Things to consider include:
> Are the joists that support the ceiling deflecting?
> Are they rotten?
> Are they undersized or too far apart?

If any of these apply, the timber floor structure may need strengthening from above. Provided the ceiling is still well adhered and sound, it is likely that it can be retained in situ (➡ Floor structures, page 106).

> Are the laths that the plaster is stuck to well fixed to the joists?
> Have the nails pulled out under the weight of the plaster?
> Have the laths rotted so they are no longer able to support the ceiling? The condition of the laths is crucial to the load-bearing capacity of the ceiling structure.

If a ceiling is deflecting, yet the joists are dead straight and the laths sound, the deflection may be the result of the plaster layer pulling away from its backing. Providing it is not a fine decorative ceiling, it may be appropriate to renew the plaster.

Repairing plaster ceilings

Holes in ceilings are common and frequently the result of water leaking from above. Although plasterers often recommend taking down the whole ceiling and

Above: When laths are sound, as they are here, holes can often be patch-repaired without replacing the entire ceiling.

Right, top: When patch-repairing old plaster, try to use like for like materials; here, water reed is used, secured under riven laths before the plaster is applied.

Right, centre: Some repairs require a little imagination and a lot of trial and error. Reed matting was used to make up the substrate in this rather tricky repair to a part-stud, part-masonry wall. Water reed proved more suitable to close the hole in the sloping ceiling.

Right, bottom: Two coats of lime plaster were then applied to the substrate, taking care to bring the final coat flush with the old plaster. The fine cracks were filled with a proprietary gypsum-based filler which allowed for sanding down prior to decorating.

replacing it with plasterboard, try to avoid this. A traditional ceiling enhances an historic interior, and plasterboard will always look flat and incongruous.

Small holes should be relatively easy to repair, either by a plasterer used to working with lime or an experienced amateur. First, cut the hole back to a rectangular shape to reveal the joists on two sides. This will allow you to fix any new laths to the existing joists. When selecting new laths to patch the hole, it is worth trying to match whatever has been used in the original ceiling. Always screw the new laths to the underside of the joists to minimise vibration and further damage. If the substrate is reed, riven laths can be used to hold it in position.

You then need to build up the plasterwork patch in two or three coats, depending on the thickness. The first coat, or 'pricking up', should be squeezed through the laths or reeds to ensure a good key (see below for plaster mixes). Ensure the pricking up coat is set back from the finished ceiling enough to allow the build-up of the other coats. Scratch the surface in a diamond pattern to allow for the next coat. For a thicker plaster ceiling, you will then need to apply a floating coat, set back just 2mm from the finished plaster ceiling. Finally, apply the setting coat and bring it flush with the existing ceiling. Allow each coat to 'carbonate' (harden) before applying the next.

Repairing wall plaster

Plaster on masonry may present a different set of problems, especially if your house has suffered damp ingress. Do not be unduly alarmed if you tap the plaster and it sounds hollow behind. Haired lime plaster is very strong and will act as a sheet, even if it has parted company with the wall itself. However, if a bulge is present in the masonry substrate, this can indicate a more serious problem relating to the structure of the house and may need further examination by a structural engineer.

Salts are another potential problem for internal plaster on external walls when a house has a history of dampness. It may be best to replace a heavily salt-laden plaster in order to produce a good final finish.

Soot staining from flues can often be seen on the plaster surface above a fireplace. When replastering such areas, a slurry of cow dung painted on to the masonry before applying the new plaster might work if the problem is not severe. If this fails to hold the staining

Right: The low-level plaster to this room had broken down due to high external ground levels. After correcting the external defect and drying out the wall, the affected areas were reinstated with a breathable two-coat lime plaster.

Below: If you own a pre-Georgian house of any quality, it is possible that early plaster layers were finished with decorative wall paintings. These are often hidden behind multiple layers of paint and patches of later plaster. Before embarking on any plaster removal, be particularly aware that you could be losing something extremely special.

Far right: A simple pargetted design typical of the east of England.

EXTERNAL FINISHES

External plasterwork, commonly known as 'render', uses largely the same techniques and materials as internal work but there are some notable types of finish.

Pargetting describes decorative exterior plasterwork frequently practised in the seventeenth century, and generally found on timber-framed buildings in the east of England. The simplest patterns were produced using sticks, sometimes with a number tied together to make a fan or a comb. Complex designs required far greater skill, and wet lime-based plaster was cast or built up layer by layer.

back, there may be no other option but to batten out the wall and apply laths and lime plaster to create a 'dry lined' finish which is isolated from the wall.

Across the country, the fashion for 'polite' architecture from the seventeenth century onwards resulted in many timber-framed buildings being smooth-rendered to conceal their 'old-fashioned' exteriors. During this period the timber-framed tradition continued but the structures had less substantial frames which were intended to be finished with a render.

Stucco was a popular finish on Georgian town houses; the term originally described plasterwork incised with lines to imitate fine stonework. This was usually executed in lime but from the late eighteenth century onwards various patented natural cements were sometimes used. Today, the term is often applied to any smooth external plastering.

Left: Stucco was used to give the impression of an expensive stone building. Here, external window surrounds are made up using in-situ moulded lime plaster.

Above right: Harling, the Scottish equivalent to roughcast, was commonly used in exposed locations. This castle sits on the edge of a ravine and its original finish remains untouched because of its inaccessibility.

Right: Pebble dash is a recent variation on roughcast, created by throwing dry pebbles or chippings on to a wet coat of smooth render. This finish was popular from Edwardian times, as seen in this example from north London.

A total contrast to stucco is roughcast, known in Scotland and northern England as 'harling'. This describes lime mixed with pea gravel thrown on to the face of the building. It was commonly used in exposed locations on the west side of the country, since its increased surface area serves to maximise evaporation and protect against driving rain.

Right: While lime plastering and rendering are relatively straightforward, certain rules have to be carefully followed. New work is particularly vulnerable to rapid drying on warm or windy days; here, repairs have been protected with damp hessian.

Opposite, top: Hair is best added to lime plaster while turning it in a mixer. The strands must be teased out and well distributed throughout the body of the mix.

Opposite, below: A 'hairy fringe' on the edge of the float or trowel is a good indicator of a well-mixed lime plaster.

NEW WORK

It is always worth trying to repair original lime plaster finishes wherever possible. However, if you are reinstating missing plaster or tackling damp, larger areas of new work using traditional materials will be necessary.

Material facts

There are no hard and fast rules when selecting the type of lime to be used for plasters and renders, although it is necessary to consider the substrate, the exposure and the time of year (➡ Lime, page 43).

Non-hydraulic (i.e. putty-based) lime render remains ideal for internal above-ground work and very soft external substrates where maximum breathability is required, including cob and wattle and daub. It is also a good choice if a building is subject to seasonal movement because it retains the greatest flexibility. However, non-hydraulic lime is particularly vulnerable to frost, and should not be applied as external render later than September, unless your plasterer can guarantee it against frost damage by undertaking additional methods of protection. Non-hydraulic lime plaster and render can be purchased ready-mixed, delivered to the site by the ton, saving space, time and money.

Hydraulic lime render is a good option for external work, particularly for exposed walls, but there will be some degree of trade-off with breathability. A feebly hydraulic lime (NHL 2) is recommended as a step up from non-hydraulic lime, and a good compromise if you are not sure. A moderately hydraulic lime (NHL 3.5) is ideal for walls that receive battering from the weather, or below ground, for instance in a basement or cellar. An eminently hydraulic lime (NHL 5) is not recommended as a render due to its limited breathability. Hydraulic lime is ideal for the repair of external cornicing and decorative detail.

PLASTER MIXES

Lime plaster and mortar are basically the same mix but plaster has the added ingredient of animal hair. This is a critical component, particularly for non-hydraulic plasters and renders, as it dramatically reduces shrinkage and cracking. Hair should be thoroughly mixed with the plaster to ensure an even distribution. Quantity is

difficult to judge, but a good guide is to take a sample on a trowel and check for an average of five hairs per centimetre.

It is always worth taking advice from an experienced plasterer as every situation is different; the plaster mixes given in the boxes (right) are typical.

Application of new lime plaster

Lime plaster will stick to most solid backgrounds; a background with a degree of suction will generally make a better substrate. Ceilings and stud walls require a background that is rigid, and allows the lime to 'key'. Riven laths are still available and provide a good substrate but are extremely expensive and very labour-intensive to fix. Expanded metal lath (EML) is often used as a substitute, although is not generally recommended. If a completely new ceiling is being constructed, and wooden lath is too expensive, a reed mat is a good alternative. Available from most lime suppliers, it comes in a roll and can be fixed with a nail gun to provide a sound, cheap substrate on which to apply a two- or three-coat lime plaster finish.

Non-hydraulic lime mix

Ideal for internal walls above ground, ceilings and externally for very soft substrates.

	Sand	Lime	Hair
SCRATCH COAT Aka pricking up coat on ceilings and rendering coat on masonry	3 parts sharp well-graded sand	1 part non-hydraulic mature lime putty (thick consistency)	Horse hair, goat hair or hay, 2kg per tonne of plaster
FLOATING COAT Aka straightening coat	3 parts sharp well-graded sand	1 part non-hydraulic mature lime putty (thick consistency)	Ideally a finer goat hair, 2kg per tonne of plaster
SETTING COAT Aka skimming coat. Note: this would usually be omitted on an external render	1 or 2 parts kiln-dried, sieved silver sand, depending on the finish required	1 part non-hydraulic mature lime putty (thick consistency)	None

Hydraulic lime mix

Ideal for external walls, cellars, basements or retaining walls. This can also be used for internal work, with or without a non-hydraulic setting coat.

	Sand	Lime	Hair
SCRATCH COAT Aka rendering coat on masonry	2½ parts sharp well-graded sand	1 part hydraulic lime NHL 2 or 3.5	Horse hair or goat hair, 2kg per tonne of plaster
FLOATING COAT Aka straightening coat	2½ parts sharp well-graded sand	1 part hydraulic lime NHL 2 or 3.5	None

Top tip: Bathrooms and kitchens

Traditionally, internal plaster would have been finished with a smooth setting coat, but using a wooden float it is possible to leave surfaces with a more open-textured, coarser coat. This finish is ideal for kitchens and bathrooms, especially when finished with a lime wash, as it will absorb excess moisture from a humid atmosphere.

Above: Reed matting is rigidly held in place using riven oak laths secured with screws or a nail gun through to the underside of the joists.

Above: The 'pricking up coat' is applied to the reed matting once it is firmly fixed in position.

Right: The pricking up coat is 'devilled' and then left to dry for a minimum of two weeks before the setting coat is applied. For a dead flat ceiling, an intermediate 'floating coat' may be necessary.

Right: The setting coat is left to firm up or 'pull in' before it can be finally trowelled up. Trowelling too early can cause the surface to bubble.

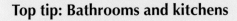

Above: An open-textured finish achieved with a wooden or plastic float will create a more vapour-permeable surface.

ROUGHCAST

This may be applied by machine but, for the average domestic house, it is often as quick to apply or 'cast' by hand. The ingredients are mixed to a sloppy, porridge-like consistency and thrown on using a dashing trowel in an action akin to hitting a tennis ball. When properly applied, with adequate pressure and at the correct angle, the mix creates a strong bond with the substrate, resulting in a longlasting finish. Roughcast is generally applied in two coats.

GETTING THE JOB DONE

Lime plasters, renders and roughcasts are notoriously difficult to apply successfully by the inexperienced. If you want to use your local plasterer but his knowledge of the material is limited, it is worth sending him on a course or employing a trainer to work alongside him on site to get him through the initial learning curve.

Lime plasters and renders work best when applied to a porous or keyed substrate. The substrate must be wetted down thoroughly in advance to control suction. To avoid drying shrinkage, especially in external work, try to slow down the 'carbonation' process.

Aftercare is critical to a successful finish. Keep renders damp with a mist spray, and cover them with damp hessian to stop moisture evaporating too quickly. It may be worth sheeting up the scaffold to shelter your new render from direct sun and drying winds. Lime renders and roughcasts will not be frost-resistant until they have carbonated back a few millimetres. Be careful not to apply them too late in the year, especially non-hydraulic renders which will take longer to go off.

If buying non-hydraulic plasters ready-mixed with hair, be sure to use them within three weeks since animal hair can dissolve due to the alkalinity of the lime. Hydraulic lime comes as dry powder in a bag; make sure it is relatively fresh and that the bag is not split.

Roughcast mix

Can be either hydraulic or non-hydraulic mixes.

	Sand	Lime	Gravel
HYDRAULIC LIME ROUGHCAST	1½ parts sharp well-graded sand	1 part hydraulic lime NHL 2 or 3.5	1 part washed pea gravel, 10mm down
NON-HYDRAULIC LIME ROUGHCAST	2 parts sharp well-graded sand	1 part non-hydraulic mature lime putty	1 part washed pea gravel, 10mm down

Right: Throwing roughcast by hand ensures the softer and less mechanical finish appropriate for an old building. Be sure to cover openings and protect any features before work starts.

Paints and finishes

Surfaces are a key element of all old buildings and the way they are finished will make or mar the overall effect. It is often better to leave well alone than to strip back the patina of age, but where redecoration is necessary choosing the right paint or finish is vital.

There is much more to traditional paints than simply historic colours. When applying a coat of paint, whether to plaster, joinery or metal, selecting the right formulation is more important than choosing the right hue or shade. Get the colour wrong and you can paint over it relatively easily. Get the paint wrong and it may peel, crack or blister, causing damage to the surface beneath, resulting in costly and time-consuming remedial work. Regardless of how much care goes into repairing an old house, it is often the use of the right paint or finish that will make all the difference to the way in which the underlying fabric will perform in the years to come.

Historic finishes have long been misunderstood, yet basic traditional paints are simple to make and easy to tint to your own colour preferences, giving a beautiful and breathable finish. They can also be bought ready-made by specialist suppliers.

In addition to original paint recipes, we are now seeing a new generation of eco-paints coming on to the market. Many are ideally suited to old buildings; gaining a proper understanding of these will be useful in making your final decisions.

Opposite: This eighteenth-century panelling was constructed out of softwood, always with the intention of covering it with paint. The fashion for stripped pine is a modern one.

Right: Like the Forth Bridge, old buildings need regular redecoration. Whether you use a professional, or carry out the work yourself, careful preparation followed by the choice of an appropriate finish is key.

Above: The texture and colour of walls impacts enormously on the general ambience of a space, with different paints reflecting light in different ways. The 'warmth' of this interior owes much to the choice of finish.

Right: Buildings were often originally finished externally with limewash. This street of limewashed houses in Corsham, Wiltshire, has survived largely intact.

Top tip: Stripped pine?

Contrary to popular belief, the 'traditional' look of stripped pine is historically inaccurate . Cheap, knotty softwoods were invariably painted or 'grained' so that the surface resembled hardwood. Only oak, mahogany and other expensive hardwoods were left exposed.

Above: The interior surfaces to this house have been meticulously prepared and decorated with traditional hand-tinted paints, giving them an extraordinary quality of finish. The chosen colours are bold, yet complementary.

TRADITIONAL PAINTS

Vernacular buildings were usually finished with simple homemade paints. The two most common types were limewash and soft distemper. These may have been applied white, or tinted. Traditional colours in vernacular buildings tended to be based around the earth pigment range, from yellow ochres through the orange and terracotta spectrum: such pigments are simply crushed earth or soft rocks.

In more costly houses, certainly from Georgian times, plaster and joinery was finished with high-quality paints based on linseed oil and lead carbonate.

By the nineteenth century, the demand for mass-produced paints produced a plethora of new patented brands and a wide range of pigments to satisfy the rising middle classes, keen to keep up with fashions. The invention of washable distempers provided a cheap and durable paint finish that satisfied the Victorian preoccupation with cleanliness.

Limewash

Limewash extends back over two thousand years and remains the ultimate breathable paint. Easily made by diluting slaked lime, it was recognised for its antiseptic qualities: farm buildings were given an annual wash with lime to maintain a clean environment. Externally, limewash was used to decorate rubble stone walls or to finish plaster.

Soft distemper

This was based on chalk dust, 'whiting', mixed with animal-skin glue size, a sticky gel made from glue dissolved in hot water. Separately, whiting was also mixed with hot water to a creamy consistency, and the two liquids were then combined. White soft distemper was a common paint for use on decorative plasterwork. Ceilings required regular redecoration because of smoke from candlelight and open fires. The dirty coat was washed right off with hot water prior to the application of a new coat, preventing paint build-up and the obscuring of detail.

Soft distemper has an opaque, chalky appearance. Although relatively breathable, it is not recommended for damp areas and is desirable for internal use only for its solubility. It can still be purchased, although it is usually mixed to order since it has a limited shelf life.

Right: The remains of limewash are still evident on this range of farm buildings in South Wales. Externally, the paint was tinted with earth pigments; internally, the walls were annually limewashed in white for sterilisation.

Below: Soft distemper is relatively breathable. Since it can be washed off, it was often used on ceilings which required regular redecoration.

Left: A cross-section of paint from joinery in a room of the 1780s, viewed under a microscope. Successive colour schemes are shown, separated by lines of dirt.

Above: Modern paints, as here, may cover two hundred years or more of earlier schemes.

Lead paints

Good-quality traditional paints were a combination of linseed oil and toxic lead carbonate; the higher the lead content, the more durable, and more expensive, the paint.

PAINT ANALYSIS

Before embarking on work involving decoration, it is worth trying to find out what the precedent was. Just as archaeologists examine layers of earth and date artefacts found within the strata, professional conservators will undertake a full analysis, involving the examination of the layers of paint, to discover and date original decorative schemes. A cross-section is studied under a microscope and samples may also be chemically tested to identify the materials used. Based on the original cost of the pigments and finishes found in the sample, the analysis may also shed light on how expensive the materials were and therefore the status of a room.

Such work is generally carried out only in the case of particularly historic or architecturally important buildings. More general research in books, old documents and museums can often provide some basic points of reference. If you take off items such as dado rails or door furniture, always look for signs of original paintwork or wallpaper underneath. If you are removing all traces of paint finishes, it is worth keeping samples of the flakes and recording them, with their locations, for future reference.

REMOVING COATINGS

Removing paint and other finishes from an old buildings or simply cleaning surfaces can, in just a few moments, destroy the patina of age and layers of history that have accumulated over hundreds of years. It is quite common to find decorative wall paintings in early houses which have been obscured by later coatings. These range from simple stencil decorations to elaborate painted scenes. If you stumble across traces of these, you should always consult your conservation officer before proceeding further; grants may be available to help preserve important decorative schemes. If you cannot afford to conserve a painting, take advice on how to cover it over to keep it intact for future generations.

Sometimes there are good reasons for removing surface coatings. For example, few paints can be applied

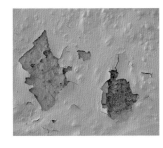

Top: The remains of this seventeenth-century wall painting in a Devon house were discovered during repair works and the surviving fragments conserved.

Above: A modern 'plastic' paint used over a breathable limewash finish will peel off. Ideally, it should be removed and the surface redecorated with limewash, which will be compatible with the substrate.

over soft distemper, since they would crack and peel off; the earlier coat should be rinsed off with warm water back to a sound substrate. A build-up of paint layers might be obscuring the fine detail of timber or plaster

Safety first

Paints applied prior to the 1970s probably contain lead. Until the 1980s, some textured wall finishes such as Artex contained asbestos. These finishes should be removed with great caution, possibly by specialist contractors.

When stripping or sanding down any previously painted surfaces, ensure that the room is well ventilated, always use high-performance dust masks and, if using a hot air gun, be particularly careful of fumes. Only work for short periods, always wash your hands and skin thoroughly after sanding down or using chemicals, and wash clothes to remove the dust. Keep children and pets away from areas where there may be a danger of dust particles or where chemicals are being used.

mouldings, or 'plastic' paints or sealants may be trapping moisture in brick or stonework. Even so, careful thought should be given to the consequences before any work is undertaken. If you think the surface you are working on is valuable in any way, always call in a specialist conservator.

The removal processes themselves, however, can cause irreversible physical damage, and the surfaces revealed by your efforts will often be inappropriate and may be hugely disappointing, especially if evidence of past repairs or damage is exposed.

When it comes to removing coatings, there are many methods but no magic formula. Most need patience and are time-consuming and labour-intensive. Every case must be evaluated individually and the gentlest method always considered first.

Before proceeding, make tests on a small, inconspicuous area and, if in doubt, do not proceed. Water and chemicals used for cleaning can soak into the fabric of a building, bring salts to the surface and cause long-term damage and erosion. When using scrapers, be careful not to dig into the underlying surface as you are stripping. Wooden or plastic spatulas and nylon bristle brushes are often preferable to coarser tools. The job may be messy, so protect the surrounding surfaces. When you have completed the removal process, it is sometimes necessary to neutralise any chemicals used.

Above: Many old paints contain lead. This is most dangerous in the form of dust when rubbing down, but also use protection against fumes when using a hot air gun.

Removal methods

A. Water-based, non-toxic, solvent-free eco-products.

B. Solvents, sold by most DIY stores. When brushed on they cause the paint to blister so that it can be scraped away; the process may have to be repeated several times.

C. Alkaline (caustic) strippers soften the paint so that it may be removed by scraper or by scrubbing with a hard brush and water. Some systems employ a fibrous blanket laid over the top which stops the stripper drying too quickly; when peeled off it takes the paint with it.

D. Poultices are effective for stubborn problems because of a prolonged contact time. A true poultice is intended to draw out deep-seated contaminants, but the term is now used to cover a wide range of cleaning materials and techniques. Clay (sepiolite or attapulgite), saturated with water, is the most common poultice medium but paper, cotton, talc,

chalk and flour are also used to draw out stains and soluble salts that may be causing decay. Alkaline poultice strippers (see C) are commonly used for paint removal.

E. Caustic baths allow entire items to be dipped, using either hot or cold systems. Hot dipping, in particular, can result in wood shrinkage and distortion; it may loosen joints and raise the grain. Never strip veneered timber this way as it is likely to delaminate.

F. Heat applied with a hot air guns helps to soften paint so that it can be scraped off but take care to avoid scorching. Fit a heat deflector near glass to prevent cracking it. The use of heat always poses a fire risk: dust, wattle and thatch are easily ignited. Great care should be taken with sash windows: the wood shavings left over in the sash boxes can smoulder undetected for some time before catching alight. Blow torches, with naked flames, should never be used.

Above left: To remove paint from brickwork, a proprietary alkaline-based paste (see C) is spread over the surface.

Above: Once applied, the paste is covered with a special fibrous tissue to prevent it from drying out. The paste reacts with the paint, softening it over a number of hours. The covering is then removed bringing the paint and paste with it. The stripped surface is then neutralise following the manufacturer's instructions.

Left: Steam wallpaper strippers are a simple and benign way of removing plastic paints which are poorly adhered to their substrate. They are not always successful, but certainly worth a try.

Right: Sandblasting can be extremely aggressive, especially on softer, weaker surfaces such as timber, soft stone and old brick. It should only ever be a last resort.

G. Steam wallpaper strippers will remove certain paints from plaster; do not allow the moisture to penetrate too deeply or it may weaken the surface.

H. Abrasive methods, such as sanding and the use of wire brushes, must be executed with considerable care. Sandblasting and high-pressure water cleaning should generally be avoided since they carry a real risk of causing irreversible damage to the fabric of a building. However, specialist systems are available using super-heated steam or fine powder which are designed to be gentle. In all cases. it is advisable to consult a conservation professional before considering any abrasive methods. Never use power tools or wire brushes, except on metalwork. When removing loose masonry paint from rubble stone, it may be possible to chip it off using a 'scutch' hammer.

Right: Thick layers of modern paint can sometimes be removed using a 'scutch' hammer. This technique is most suitable on rubble stone; it can cause damage to fine surfaces such as ashlar and brick.

Removal from timber

Possible removal methods: A, B, C, D, E, F.

Caustic soda dissolved in water will often remove tar and linseed oil. Dipping should be considered a last resort for timber items; question any firm you propose to use closely about their methods and the likely condition of items following the process.

Warnings

> Never sandblast or use other abrasive methods on old beams. They will quickly destroy the surface, especially if the timber has been subjected to beetle attack; mouldings and other historic detail may also be lost.

> Avoid using wire wool on oak, since it can stain the wood.

> Hardwoods can become darker or change colour with certain chemicals.

> Excessive water or scrubbing will raise the grain of all timber.

Removal from brick and stone

Possible removal methods: A, B, C, D, H.

Removing paint completely from these substrates is difficult; although bricks and stones may appear hard, they are easily damaged. Bricks have an outer protective skin, formed during the firing process, which is easily destroyed, with the result that water penetration will be encouraged, in turn leading to spalling and the ingress of dirt. Often it is advisable to seek the help of a specialist company who will select the appropriate method for the job and deal with the care and removal of any toxic chemicals involved. In some cases, although it is unsightly, the best solution may be to let paint peel off naturally over time. For stone or brick floors, a range of proprietary cleaners are available. Mastic adhesives can usually be removed with specialist solvents but, as with all stone or brickwork, great care should be taken.

Warnings

> Never use wire brushes or sanding.

> Other abrasive methods should be undertaken only by highly competent conservation professionals, since any damage to the surface of brick or stone will speed up future erosion.

> Chemicals may react with stone – for example, acidic products can dissolve limestone and marble. Where chemicals are used, ensure that they are subsequently neutralised.

Above: One system employs superheated steam to 'melt' modern plastic paints. It uses minimum water and is gentle, minimising damage to the substrate. It is successful only in certain situations, however, so arrange a trial prior to use.

Above right: The outer protective skin of bricks is easily destroyed by sandblasting, spoiling their appearance and leaving them vulnerable to water penetration and spalling.

> Avoid water saturation, which may bring harmful salts to the surface.

> Never use methods involving water when there is likely to be a frost.

Removal from marble

Possible removal methods: A, B, C, D.

Marble is easily damaged. It should not be confused with vulnerable scagliola, plasterwork coloured to imitate marble. Poultices of attapulgite clay or white paper kitchen towel soaked in distilled water may remove some paints and stains.

Warnings

> Some strippers damage marble, so check the manufacturer's instructions.
> Never use abrasive methods.

Removal from plaster

Possible removal methods: A, B, C, D, G.

Size-bound (soft) distemper should wash off with warm water; a little added wallpaper stripper may help. Steam strippers can be effective for other paints.

Warnings

> Avoid digging into plaster with scraper blades.
> Avoid penetration by excessive moisture.
> Ensure that any chemicals are neutralised.

Removal from metalwork

Possible removal methods: A, B, C, D, E, H.

Loose paint and rust may be removed from iron and steel using wire brushes, abrasive paper or wire wool. Chemical paint removers are often effective in removing built-up layers of paint that are obscuring surface detail. An old toothbrush can be useful where fine patterns are involved. Clean off metalwork with a rag dipped in white spirit rather than water to prevent rust, and prime or treat with a chemical rust inhibitor immediately.

Warnings

> Aluminium, lead and other soft metals must be treated with care, so avoid abrasive methods.

DECORATING SYSTEMS
External wall surfaces

Do not be deceived by the new generation of so-called 'microporous' paints which promise great things. Many of these still prevent surfaces from breathing in a traditional manner. Even water-based systems are no guarantee of permeability, and many contain plastic compounds that lock in the damp. Limewash remains the king of external paints, and no modern equivalent can beat it in terms of breathability, durability, economy or ease of application.

Limewash step-by-step

To make the limewash

You will need: a clean plastic dustbin with lid, lime putty, water, cordless electric drill with a plasterer's whisk attachment, steel trowel, goggles.

> Pour the clean water into the dustbin.
> Add the lime putty, roughly in the proportion of 1:3 parts putty to water.
> Wearing goggles, combine the water and putty using the whisk.
> Test the consistency of the mix by dipping in the steel trowel, which must be clean. The ideal mix will form a definite line across the top of the trowel but will still be translucent against the grey steel. It should be the thickness of semi-skimmed milk.

> If the mix is too thin, add a little more putty; if it is too thick, add more water.
> Keep it covered with the dustbin lid. Limewash should have a good shelf life, although it will settle after a few weeks and will require re-mixing before use.
> The above will produce white limewash. For colours, ➠ Hints on tints, page 174.

To prepare the wall

You will need: polythene sheeting, gaffer tape, stiff bristle brush.

> Erect a suitable and safe working platform, set back a little from the wall surface.
> Carry out any necessary repairs to the wall before limewashing.
> Mask any windows, doors and other details to protect from splatters.
> Protect the ground at the base of the wall as necessary.
> Using a stiff brush, remove any loose particles from the surface of the wall.
> Remove any lichen or mould growth from the surface with an appropriate fungicide.

To apply the limewash

You will need: hosepipe and water spray, clean bucket, goggles, surgical gloves, short-haired block brush, smaller brush for 'cutting in'.

> The key to a sound, dustproof, limewash finish is to apply thin coats to a damp surface and to slow down the rate of 'carbonation', i.e. drying out. The ideal weather for limewashing is therefore a mild, drizzly day. On a sunny day, consider the orientation of the building: do not, for example, tackle the east elevation until the afternoon, when the sun will have moved around. Direct sunlight will dry limewash out too quickly.

> Thoroughly wet the substrate before application. Ideally, this should be done with a hosepipe with a mist spray attachment and trigger; alternatively, you can use a good-quality pump-action mist spray. A simple hand-held spray will not be powerful enough.
> Working from the top down, wet up again about a square metre of wall, then apply the limewash to the damp surface.

> Work the limewash into the crevices of the wall surface using a block-brush.
> Do not worry if the limewash appears to be very thin – it is better to apply thin coats than thick ones.

> As the limewash absorbs carbon dioxide from the atmosphere, it will become lighter and more opaque.
> Allow 24 hours between coats. Re-wet the wall thoroughly before the next application. Repeat the operation for the remaining coats.

Limewash

> Limewash likes to stick to porous surfaces, ideally brick, stone and lime plaster or roughcast.

> Limewash is not durable on non-porous surfaces such as cement renders, masonry paints and hard modern bricks.

> Five thin coats are usually sufficient for new plaster or bare brick or stone.

> When applied to a porous substrate, limewash will usually last a year for every coat applied, plus a couple more in a sheltered situation. Five thin coats can easily last seven years.

> Three coats may suffice to freshen up previously limewashed surfaces.

Internal wall surfaces

Internal wall surfaces in old buildings invariably take a great deal of time to prepare prior to decoration, but this pays dividends when it comes to the quality of the finish.

At the very least, gently remove all loose and flaking surfaces using a sharp-edged stripping knife. For a first-class job, remove any modern vinyl emulsion. Where this has been applied over an earlier distemper or lime-wash, it may lift off relatively easily using a wallpaper steamer. Other patches of modern paint may be impossible to remove, especially those applied over patches of gypsum plaster. It may be advisable to rub down previously emulsioned surfaces to provide a key.

You will often be left with a wall that is a patchwork of lime plaster, modern gypsum plaster repairs, holes, cracks and well-adhered patches of paint. This may look extremely uneven but can easily be made good. Large areas of damage should be filled with lime plaster, but small cracks and holes can be filled with a proprietary powder-based filler mixed with water. Ensure that the filler you select can be sanded down. Using a wide filling knife, work across the wall filling all holes, steps and cracks; then leave it for 24 hours before sanding.

Limewash is ideal for use internally on lime plaster on a damp wall that is still drying out. In such circumstances, limewash is the only paint that can cope with the high levels of moisture evaporation. However, due to its milky consistency and multiple-layer application, it can be time-consuming and messy to apply, particularly to ceilings! Limewash will stick only to a porous substrate and gives a blotchy finish, which may or may not be desired.

Right: Once old walls and ceilings have been prepared, the application of paint will quickly unify them. The walls to this room have been painstakingly stripped of modern paints and the surfaces filled and sanded.

Below right: Three coats of limewash were applied. The first coat was left white; the subsequent two coats were pigmented. Limewash appears transparent as it is applied, but dries to an opaque finish within a few hours.

Other paints may be preferable for dry situations. A whole range of eco-paints is available, categorised into water-, mineral- or plant-based. The water-based paints claim to be free of nasty solvents, but tend to contain chemicals such as drying agents which may devalue their green credentials. When choosing a compatible paint for a breathable substrate, check its resistance to water-vapour permeability. This is a relative concept; any paint claiming to be microporous or breathable should be compared with limewash, which will almost certainly be considerably more permeable. Clay-based emulsions and casein paints are preferable to modern emulsions for unifying a wall made up of a patchwork of repairs.

An alternative to eco-paints are 'contract emulsions'. These are basically emulsions that do not contain vinyl, and therefore have greater permeability and a matt finish with no sheen. They are a good option if painting over modern paint finishes, but are not advised as a finish to new lime plaster.

Right: Natural and 'eco' paints are far more pleasant to use than paints containing solvents and other chemicals.

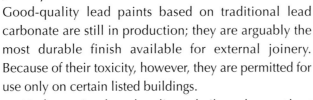

Joinery

Good-quality lead paints based on traditional lead carbonate are still in production; they are arguably the most durable finish available for external joinery. Because of their toxicity, however, they are permitted for use only on certain listed buildings.

Modern paints based on linseed oil are the next best thing to traditional lead paints. These are eco-friendly and can be blended for a greater colour palette. They are best applied to either sound lead paint or bare wood surfaces in order to gain the full benefit of the paint. These paints vary, but it is common practice to use raw linseed oil as a primer. This can either be applied hot, by warming it on a stove prior to application, or applied cold and then heated up with a hot air gun in situ.

Linseed-oil paints should be applied in very thin layers, otherwise they simply form a skin on the surface and remain soft beneath. Allow each layer to dry thoroughly, and lightly sand down between coats. Three thin layers will usually suffice. Linseed-oil paints take longer to dry than most of today's 'plastic' paints and should not be applied in cold, damp weather.

Above: Ideally, joinery should be stripped back to bare wood before redecorating in order to achieve a sound finish. Old paints are likely to contain lead and should be removed with caution.

Right: Linseed oil paint is best applied to bare wood in very thin layers, and allowed to dry thoroughly before sanding down ready for the next coat.

Hints on tints

Your local lime supplier will sell a wide variety of pigments in powder form, varying in price from cheap earth-based pigments to more expensive mineral-based colours. If you live in an area with rich coloured soils, for instance the bright red earths of Devon, why not experiment by making your own pigments? Simply crush the earth or clay – the finer the powder, the richer the colour.

To blend pigments successfully, mix them with warm water in a jam jar. Screw the lid on tightly and shake well. Pigments in solution can be blended with most water-based paints, including limewashes, modern emulsions, casein and clay paints, even modern masonry paints. If you need to unify a wall that is part lime render and part cement render, try using limewash on the breathable surfaces and masonry paint, with the same pigments, on the non-porous cement surfaces.

Test the colour by applying it to a sheet of white card. Wet and dry paint differ in colour, so allow paint to dry in order to gauge the final effect.

Above: Pigments may be blended with most water-based paints, allowing you to create exactly the hue you require. Better-quality, more finely ground pigments are less likely to 'streak'.

Warning: spontaneous combustion Waste rags used with linseed oil or other flammable decorating materials must either be destroyed or laid out to dry quite flat. If they are left balled up they may catch fire.

Internal oak beams

For previously untreated beams, remove dust and dirt with a damp cloth or a soft brush; if a light sheen is required, apply a thin coat of beeswax polish. To consolidate soft or wormy patches, beeswax diluted with turpentine can be applied with a brush and, once dry, buffed with a soft cloth. Although linseed oil is often suggested as a finish, being slightly sticky it attracts dust and dirt and discolours over time. To lighten dark oak beams, try using a proprietary liming wax or, for an opaque finish, casein-based paint.

Floor finishes

As with all surfaces, it is important not to destroy the patina of age when caring for timber floors, but they may be coated with unattractive layers of dirt which need to be removed. If the problem is particularly bad, scrub the floors in the direction of the grain with warm soapy water and a stiff bristle brush. Rinse with clean water as you go, and pick up excess moisture with a towel to prevent it from sitting on the boards. With any treatment involving water, use the minimum amount to prevent lifting the grain. Excess polish can be removed from a wooden floor with white spirit.

Linseed oil is not recommended for floorboards any more than for beams. The traditional finish for oak and elm boards is home-made beeswax polish. Where a floor is taking a lot of traffic, it may be better to use a proprietary blended beeswax that contains a hardener, such as carnauba wax, for greater durability. Wax is not

Making beeswax polish

Beeswax polish can be made simply by taking a lump of beeswax, grating it into a jam jar and covering it with pure turpentine. Leave it to stand overnight and then shake well. The turps dissolves the wax to produce a good polish.

If you have worm holes, make the wax to a thinner consistency so that it can be brushed into the wood; this helps to consolidate the damaged timber. Use less turps to create a stiff polish for waxing with a soft cloth. Several coats may be required. Both beeswax and turps are generally available from old-fashioned hardware stores.

Top: Casein paint provides an opaque finish and is one means of lightening dark oak beams and boards.

Second from top: Beeswax polish gives life back to floorboards. Buffing regularly will bring back the shine.

Above: Graining on a door discovered when stripping twentieth-century paint from the door of a farmhouse.

Above right: Always save fragments of wallpaper and paint if you discover them.

a one-off treatment; fresh coats will need to be applied occasionally to maintain the floor. Never apply thick coats of wax in an attempt to achieve quick results: it will remain soft, hold the dirt and look dull. Regularly sweep or vacuum floors to remove grit and dirt which will cause scratching. To bring back the shine, buff with a soft cloth or a mechanical floor polisher (➡ Maintaining brick and stone, page 114).

Wallpapers

Remarkably, old wallpaper sometimes survives, occasionally complete or as hidden fragments, often behind skirtings, architraves or built-in cupboards. If you are redecorating, try to preserve a fragment because it provides an insight into the past decoration of the building. If removed, pieces of original wallpaper should be kept in dry conditions, flat between sheets of acid-free paper; always record which room they came from and where.

Wallpaper glue is not very breathable, so paper is not advised for walls that have suffered from damp: the paper will hinder the drying-out process and peel off.

Graining

With the advent of cheap softwoods from the eighteenth century, a fashion developed for 'graining', applying paint to give the appearance of an expensive hardwood. Traces of original graining can often be found, particularly in Victorian and Edwardian houses. Specialist decorators are able to replicate such schemes using graining brushes; if you are artistic, you may also be able to achieve an acceptable finish with a little tuition.

Building services

Old buildings present challenges when it comes to what we regard as the essentials of life. Mains drainage, running water, gas and electricity were unheard of when some homes were built. Try to incorporate these services without spoiling historic character.

Of all the building services, foul water and rainwater drainage were incorporated first. By the eighteenth century, the rising middle classes were devising ever more innovative ways of servicing their homes; the first patent for a water closet was in 1775. The invention of the incandescent gas mantle in 1885 started a revolution, taken forward by the Edwardians who began to establish electricity as the main means of lighting.

Finding an array of servants' bells always causes excitement and fascination, but items such as Bakelite switches are all too easily disregarded, often seeming of no value. In reality, all the service elements from the past provide fascinating glimpses of a building's history; they should be retained wherever possible.

Incorporating new services into an old house is a challenge that most people involved in a building project will have to address. Houses change hands much faster than in the past, and the facilities within them are constantly being updated as technology and fashion change. With this in mind, try to plan your services so that they can be removed or altered easily in the future without damaging the building.

RAINWATER SYSTEMS

Maintaining gutters and downpipes is crucial to the wellbeing of your home: faulty or inadequate rainwater systems or leaking drains are responsible for the majority of damp problems in old buildings. To ensure that water does not run down the face of the building or collect at the base of the walls, an effective rainwater system must have the capacity to cope with the heaviest downpour.

Gutters are designed to empty into downpipes, either directly or via a hopper. In turn, the downpipe discharges, often via a gulley, into a drain which usually runs to the boundary of the plot where it connects to a public sewer. Alternatively, rainwater disposal may be via a soakaway, dug some distance from the building, or a natural watercourse. With any system, it is worth thinking about conserving at least some rainwater by

Above: Servants' bells are one of the most fascinating and visible service elements in a house, conjuring an instant link with a bygone era. They give a clue to the status of the house and, if the bell pulls or pushes are still present, to the individual rooms.

connecting a butt to a downpipe – but do ensure that this has an overflow that carries excess water away from your home.

Maintenance

Leaking or overflowing rainwater systems can cause damp, rot or even subsidence, so you ignore their maintenance at your peril. Inspect your entire rainwater system at least once a year – November is a good time because the leaves have fallen. Regular maintenance often involves nothing more than clearing gutters and gullies and checking for leaks.

Gutters and thatch

Thatch is the exception to the rule, and may have no gutter. Instead, it has very wide eaves that are designed to shed water clear of the wall. If you are concerned about waterlogged soil where the rainwater lands, a French drain, in line with the rainwater run-off, may be a good solution (➥ French drains, page 38).

Above: Thatched properties rarely have gutters and, where they do, installation is never easy. In this case, the gutter is of wood, possibly lined with lead, and the water is shot away from the building without the aid of a downpipe. The wide overhang means that special brackets have had to be made to hold the gutter in place.

Top: Poorly maintained rainwater systems provide the ideal growing environment for buddleia and other plants.

Above: This brickwork bears testament to the damage caused by long-term water leakage from gutters, hopper heads and downpipes.

Assessing the condition

> Stains or moss on walls and plant growth around downpipes are indicators of trouble.
> Wait for a heavy rainstorm and observe the performance of your rainwater goods.
> Check for leaks. Use a mirror to inspect the backs of downpipes and gutters. Look for poor or damaged joints, rusted bolts and fittings and rotten fascia boards. With leadwork, look for signs of cracking or distortion.
> Ensure that there are no blockages that might cause water to spill from the tops of pipes or, if trapped, to freeze, causing cracks and splits in the metalwork.
> Gutters should be adequately supported on brackets to cope with the weight of snow. They must also be laid to a sufficient fall: check this by pouring in a bucket of water at the high end of their length.
> Gutters and pipes that are too small will not cope in a heavy downpour. For sizing advice, calculate the approximate area of your roof and speak to a gutter manufacturer.

Above: Roof valleys and hopper heads are both troublesome areas if not properly maintained. This is a clear example of what can occur if they are allowed to become blocked with debris or are damaged.

Top tip: Avoiding blockages

> Pipe 'balloons' should be fitted at the top of downpipes to stop debris entering the system.
> Ideally, downpipes should be fitted with a shoe at their base discharging above the gulley grille. This allows for easy inspection and maintenance.
> Gullies should be protected with a cover that can be easily lifted.
> A hidden roof valley can be particularly problematic during snow; consider installing electric trace heating tapes in hard-to-reach places to avoid ice build-up.

Left: Ensuring that rainwater downpipes and gullies can run freely is essential and should be part of a regular maintenance routine.

Installation and decorating

Rainwater systems require different methods of installation. Product manufacturers will normally offer advice on the components required and on how they should be assembled, but there are certain key points to consider.

When fitting gutters make sure that enough brackets are used to support the additional weight of water or snow. Always ensure the gutter has sufficient fall to work efficiently. If fixing to a fascia, check that the timber is sound, otherwise the weight of rainwater may cause it to collapse. Avoid fitting a fascia to an old building where none has existed previously as it can look out of place; instead, fit gutter brackets to the rafter ends or wall. Cast iron downpipes should be set off the wall by at least

25mm to make redecoration possible and to ensure that water does not soak into the building if the pipe becomes cracked or blocked.

Cast iron quickly rusts if left undecorated. Rust on existing parts should be cleaned with a wire hand-brush or a rotary wire cup-brush on a power drill, then painted appropriately as soon as possible. New cast iron sections are available with a factory-applied finished coating. If they are uncoated, or you are re-using old sections, they need to be painted prior to fixing; pay particular attention to the backs of downpipes and gutters. Black bituminous paint should be used on the insides of gutters and hopperheads.

Bringing services to your home

> Decide what services you will need and plan routes for them at the earliest opportunity.
> When digging trenches for pipes or cables, be mindful of any underground archaeology, including old drainage systems; if possible, record their position.
> Where external cobbles or flagstones exist, carefully set them to one side before disturbing the ground so that they may be reinstated.
> Consider the aesthetic impact of poles, overhead lines and satellite dishes. In some cases, listed building consent may be required. Enquire about burying cables where possible.

Above: Digging trenches for underground pipework carries a risk of subsidence or collapse.

Above: Services are rarely attractive. This mains electrical cable was later buried underground.

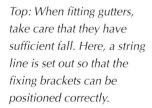

Top: When fitting gutters, take care that they have sufficient fall. Here, a string line is set out so that the fixing brackets can be positioned correctly.

Above: Water run-off from the roof must fall into gutters without overshooting or running down the back into the fascia.

Rainwater goods: material facts

Ideally rainwater goods should be replaced like-for-like using historical precedent; where a change is required, there are key points to consider.

Pros	Cons
Lead Attractive natural patina and does not require painting Virtually maintenance free if fitted correctly Long-lasting	Downpipes are fixed tight to the wall to prevent movement, a disadvantage in that leaks will almost certainly seep into the building Repairs need to be carried out by specialist leadworkers Can split, crack or sag
Cast iron Aesthetically pleasing Long-lasting and strong Not easily damaged by ladders or weight of snow Profiles have changed little with time, so sections are easily replaced Bolts into place Can be purchased pre-painted	Corrodes and needs regular redecoration Heavy and requires careful fixing
Cast aluminium Available in similar sections to cast iron and can serve as a substitute Light in weight and easy to fix Long-lasting, strong and not easily damaged Does not corrode, so needs less regular redecoration Can be purchased powder-coated in a variety of colours Recyclable	Not traditional Lacks the texture of cast iron
Copper Attractive natural patina and does not require painting Works well with modern extensions to historic buildings Lightweight, strong and long-lasting Recyclable	Not traditional
Plastic Cheap and easy to fix	Lacks the aesthetic qualities of traditional materials Prone to distortion May rattle and creak Rarely acceptable on listed buildings

Above: Decorative detailing was frequently added to lead downpipes and hopper heads. This example of a new downpipe clearly shows the beauty of the material.

Above: The profiles of cast iron rainwater goods have changed little with time. This new cast iron downpipe and shoe sit happily against the wall of an old building.

Above: The swan neck of this cast aluminium downpipe lacks the surface texture of cast iron, but is similar in section, easy to maintain and lightweight.

DRAINAGE

Drains are easily forgotten until there is a problem. Blockages, fractured pipes and inefficient septic tanks may lead to unpleasant smells as well as subsidence, low-level damp and heave, not to mention health hazards. Therefore it is worth investigating where the wastewater goes and how efficient the system is.

A simple test it to lift manhole covers and then run water from the taps and WCs within the property, observe where it flows and whether it runs freely. Testing for leaks and blockages involves plugging the drain at the lower end, filling it up with water, and then waiting to see if the water is held or if it leaks away. When the plug is removed, the water should flow away rapidly to indicate that the drain is not blocked.

One of the problems with older properties is that there may be few or no inspection chambers. In these cases, the only way to check the drains is to dig down to the pipes and break into them. If in doubt, arrange for a professional drainage survey; this may involve the use of a small CCTV camera passed through the drains to pinpoint any problems. Should you need to change your drainage system, speak to your building control officer first as you must comply with building regulations.

Left: Copper is left in its natural state so saves the need for regular repainting. This newly installed gutter will soon mellow, taking on an attractive patina which works well with modern extensions to old buildings.

Left: Plastic guttering can be a cheap and useful temporary solution, but lacks the aesthetic qualities of traditional materials and is rarely acceptable on old buildings.

Below: The 'brushes' which help guide and protect the specially designed CCTV camera have been removed here to allow it to fit into the pipe.

Below: Images from the camera are fed to a small TV screen, enabling the operator to locate damage or obstructions such as tree roots within the drain.

Top tip: Before you buy

When buying an old house, consider the cost and maintenance implications of dealing with drainage systems. Septic tanks, cesspools and other sewage treatment systems will need to be maintained and emptied regularly. Try to ascertain if there are any drains running under the house and whether a drainage plan exists. Enquire whether there have been any drainage problems and when the drains were last checked.

Left: Septic tanks or other sewage treatment systems are major items. Plan for where they will be sited, the work involved in burying them underground and the routing of the drainage system linked to them.

Drainage systems

In older properties, the waste pipes may be formed of lead or cast iron and are divided into two separate systems. The lavatories (foul water) feed directly into a large-bore soil pipe which leads to the underground drains; waste from such items as baths and sinks empties along smaller pipes into open hoppers atop vertical pipes that discharge into drainage gullies at ground level. Since the 1960s, a single-stack system has generally been employed, meaning that all water drains into the same vertical soil pipe.

In both systems, foul smells from the sewer are prevented from escaping by the use of traps in the pipework which remain full of water. To prevent this being siphoned out and allow gases to escape, a soil pipe vents to the open air above the eaves, fitted with a cage to prevent birds nesting. Alternatively, an air admittance valve may be used within the property, often in the loft or eaves space.

Clay pipes have traditionally been employed for drainage underground; these are accessed via brick-built inspection chambers. The last in the line before the main

Top: Inspection chambers were generally built of brick and often rendered on the inside. A semicircular section of clay pipe runs through the base and is connected to clay pipes on either side.

Above: Modern plastic drainage pipes are relatively simple to lay and should be bedded in pea shingle to allow for movement.

Right: Cable routes should be carefully planned to avoid marring the outside of a building.

Far right: Old switches, sockets and cables are signs that an electrical system may need to be replaced.

sewer should have an interceptor trap as a barrier to smells and rats. A cleaning eye or stopper above the trap allows blockages to be cleared using drain rods. Clay pipes can cause problems when new sections are connected; make sure your builder understands how best to make connections and has allowed for this in any estimate.

Modern pipes and drainage systems are made of plastic, and inspection chambers are prefabricated, making them much easier to install than in the past, but care must still be taken to ensure sufficient fall on pipes to carry the water away. Drainage systems are subject to building control (➡ Building control, page 24).

ELECTRICAL INSTALLATIONS

Old or inadequate wiring poses a real safety and fire risk, so an essential first step is to establish the quality of the existing electrical installation. A qualified electrician should check systems at least every ten years since cables, switches, sockets and other accessories deteriorate over time.

The type of sockets and light switches employed may give a clue to the age of an installation, but do not be deceived by modern fittings connected to old wiring. Rubber-coated cables were last fitted in the 1960s; those coated in lead or fabric are even older. New wiring colours – blue for neutral; brown for live, and green-and-yellow for earth – replaced black and red colour coding in March 2004, and became compulsory two years later. Antiquated fuse boards with a wooden back and cast iron switches are another indication of the need for rewiring.

Modern electrical systems, designed to offer high levels of protection against shock, are fed from a distribution board known as a consumer unit. This incorporates a manual means of isolating the incoming supply as well as circuit breakers and RCDs (residual current

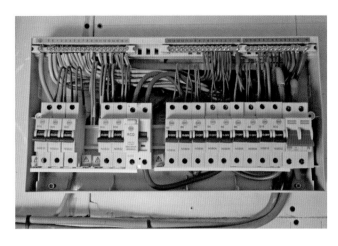

> Try to avoid running electrical cables in the roof space. A thatched roof in particular can provide a haven for mice which frequently gnaw cables, often resulting in fire.

Choosing cables

Select the most appropriate type of cable, which is going to give long life, maximum safety and allow future expansion of the system: this will avoid unnecessary future damage and disruption to the building. Factors such as vermin attack, damage from ultra-violet light, heat and abrasion all need to be taken into account and discussed in advanced with your electrician.

PVC-sheathed cable is the most commonly used. Other cables can provide added levels of safety and durability, particularly in areas such as roof spaces.

devices), which automatically interrupt the flow of electrical current if the circuit develops a fault. They will dramatically reduce the risk of an electrical fire or electric shock. Any outdated distribution board should be upgraded at the earliest opportunity.

Planning ahead

If you are rewiring a house, a great deal of planning and preparation is required.

> Always use a NICEIC-approved electrician and explain the need for sensitivity and care.
> 'First fix' electrical works – installation of cables and back boxes – must be carried out early, before plastering, flooring and decoration.
> Draw up a floor plan and mark the position of your furniture; then add the position of light fittings, power sockets and switches, along with TV, radio, telephone and internet connectivity.
> Never underestimate how many power sockets or light fittings you might need. It is far cheaper and less damaging to the building to install them when a property is being rewired than to add them later, and much safer than using adapters and trailing leads. Remember to include supplies to boilers and cabling for applicances such as thermostats.
> Beware of using old switches, fuseboards and other electrical equipment in your new installation; they are unlikely to meet today's safety standards. If appropriate, disconnect them but leave them in position as part of the history of the property.
> At the end of the job, the system should be fully tested and an electrical installation certificate obtained, meeting the requirements of the current building regulations.

Choosing sockets and switches

> Think about where you want your sockets and switches and mark the exact position in pencil on your wall. Electricians have a tendency to place them in visually obtrusive positions!
> Think about hiding ugly sockets behind hinged skirting boards.
> Do not be restricted by standard white plastic fittings – there are many other options, from reproduction Bakelite to modern stainless steel. Architrave switches are specially designed to fit narrow spaces.

HOME TECHNOLOGY

With technology changing fast, it is important to make sure any wiring is accessible and can be adapted in the future without damage to the building. Where possible, consider wireless solutions. Plan for telephone sockets

Above left: The consumer unit is at the heart of a modern electrical system, with circuit breakers to allow individual circuits to be isolated.

Above: Damage caused by mice can result in an electrical fire.

Right: 'Second fix' occurs after the 'wet trades', such as plastering, are finished.

Far right: Bakelite switches can still be sourced and will often be in keeping with the aesthetics of an old house.

Lighting

Illuminating an old property is a challenge, and just as important a consideration as paint colours and furnishings.

> Try to select your fittings before your electrician starts – he will need to fix the cable in a position to suit. Once plasterwork has been made good, alterations are difficult.

> Where ceilings are low, the light from table lamps can be highly effective. They can be run from 2 or 5 amp sockets, enabling them to be switched on from the main entry light switch.

> Low-voltage lighting can be amazingly effective and is compact in size, but think before recessing it into original ceilings. Not only will you damage the fabric of the building and breach the fire resistance of the ceiling but, more importantly, the transformers and lamps give off heat and can present a fire risk in confined spaces where dust and old timber are present.

> Do not be nervous about choosing contemporary fittings – these can work extremely well in old buildings and be less obtrusive than the more traditional alternatives.

Above: These kitchen light fittings have been chosen to be as unobtrusive as possible yet provide a level of illumination in line with today's expectations.

Minimising damage

> Wherever possible, avoid knocking holes in walls or chasing plasterwork for cables or pipes; ensure that making good is done with appropriate materials. Beware of chasing lath and plaster or wattle and daub, because the structure of the wall can collapse.

> Re-using existing conduits or pipework for cabling can save considerable disruption. Old buildings often contain voids, disused chimneys and the like which can accommodate services.

> In some circumstances, it is preferable to run new pipes and cable conduits on the surface so that they are accessible and the fabric of the building is not damaged. An alternative may be to box them in.

Left: Surface-mounted socket and conduits can add to the 'feel' of a building while avoiding damage to the walls.

> Avoid floorboards being lifted repeatedly by different trades for the installation of services.

> If a floor has to be lifted, the work should be done by a carpenter in conjunction with the plumber or electrician; all involved must understand the importance of the floor. Non-powered hand tools should always be used.

> Where boards may be taken up again in the future, it is better to use brass screws than nails. This is also the answer when working above delicate plaster ceilings which might be damaged by hammering.

> Wherever possible, run pipes parallel to and between floor joists. Cutting notches in joists to accommodate pipes and cables seriously weakens floors and should be avoided; seek advice from a structural engineer if in doubt.

> Keep a diagram of all the service routes and provide access wherever possible to allow for future maintenance.

Top: Try to avoid passing pipework or cabling through walls or other parts of the building's fabric. Where it is unavoidable, keep damage to a minimum and make good with appropriate materials.

Above: Where cables have to be threaded through joists, drill holes through the centre of the timbers to minimise the weakening effect.

and television and radio aerials to be installed by an electrician along with other electrical work.

Aerials and satellite dishes

Installers usually want to locate aerials and satellite dishes in the place most convenient for them. Think about how such devices may affect the building's aesthetics. Avoid installations on main elevations, and bear in mind how cable runs might deface the facade of your home. It may be possible to site them in loft space or in the garden away from the house and still achieve good reception.

Fixing aerials to the structure of your home, particularly to the chimneys, can be damaging. With historic roofs be aware of the potential for harm caused by contractors.

Fire and security systems

Modern alarm systems can do far more than warn of intruders; they are capable of alerting you to fire and the presence of carbon monoxide. When connected to the alarm company's monitoring service via a telephone line, they can call the fire brigade to your home as quickly as possible even if it is unoccupied. This may make the difference between saving the historic fabric and losing everything, particularly if thatch is involved.

Alarm systems must be installed with sensitivity for the building's fabric. Always talk through the installation process with the company before signing a contract and, if possible, coordinate it with other work. Investigate whether a wireless system will work for you.

Smoke alarms, preferably mains-powered and linked to one another, are vital in any home to ensure the safety of you and your family. In thatched properties, in particular, install a hard-wired smoke alarm in your roof space in a place where it can be easily maintained.

LIGHTNING PROTECTION

The purpose of a lighting conductor is to direct a lightning strike to earth safely without harm to the building or its occupants; generally, more than one conductor is required. Thought needs to be given not just to the design and installation of an effective system, but one that is unobtrusive. Choice of the materials is critical, as is the position of the conductors in relation to architectural features. Think about what may be under the surface before the electrodes are driven into the ground

Top: Original windows and a modern satellite dish sit uneasily alongside each other. It may be possible to site the dish more discreetly.

Above: It is not only church spires that need lightning conductors: tall chimneys on houses are also in danger.

Right: Surface-mounted copper pipes need not look unattractive if run tidily; they save unnecessary damage to the building as well as installation time.

at the base of the building. Inspection and testing of the system must be carried out annually and after a strike.

PLUMBING

Water leaking within a building from pipes or sanitary ware is hugely damaging; even a small leak over a long period may result in rot. Be sure to repair dripping taps as soon as possible, maintain good seals around baths and showers and, in case of emergency, make sure you know the location of the main stopcock. If washers in old taps need replacing, use a plumber who appreciates their value. For a few days after any plumbing work has been undertaken, look out for leaks on new joints on both water and waste pipes.

Hot and cold water tanks should be insulated. Pipes, both in the loft and under suspended floors, must be lagged against cold. Gaps around pipes that pass through external walls need to be plugged with lime mortar.

Original plumbing often consists of lead pipework which, wherever possible, should be retained for waste and vent pipes; it is no longer acceptable for drinking water, which today passes through copper or plastic. Plastic pipes have the advantage of flexibility, so are more easily threaded through awkward spaces; their push-fit joints mean that the use of a blow torch is not required, thus minimising the risk of fire.

Make sure your plumber fits an easily accessible isolation valve to all pipes attached to every basin, WC and bath, so that you can turn off the water supply in specific places if there is a problem. When installing a new water tank or bath, think about their weight when full of water; if necessary, provide supports that are independent of the roof or ceiling structure.

The golden rule of designing new plumbing systems is to provide adequate access. Concealed cisterns, traps and wastes will inevitably need periodic maintenance.

Before work starts, confirm where the pipes will run and how they can be concealed. Most plumbers simply expect to box in pipework but this can be visually intrusive and pose a problem if things go wrong. It is worth designing the system so that joints and other weak points are not above any sensitive historic fabric, such as decorative plaster ceilings.

GAS

The servicing and fitting of gas appliances may only be carried out by CORGI-registered installers. It is a requirement to have a vent in any room with a gas appliance. Where early gas light fittings have survived, they should be retained and the possibility of making them safe and workable explored.

HEATING

Until relatively recently, open fires provided the only heat in the home – in some cases, they still do. Today, we generally demand much greater levels of warmth than in the past. Central heating may be fed by a solid fuel, oil, gas or electric boiler or kitchen range. Systems can be wet, using water to feed radiators or underfloor heating pipes, or dry, using electricity to supply storage heaters or underfloor heating cables or to circulate air via ducts and vents.

Boilers and radiators

Modern radiators are generally made of pressed steel or aluminium, while pumps allow water to circulate much more quickly than in earlier systems. As a consequence,

Top: A contemporary-style bathroom can suit an old house, especially if you can conceal cisterns and pipework (left). Make sure there is sufficient and easy access to it for maintenance.

Above: Your gas meter is the property of the gas company. If it needs to be moved or altered, allow plenty of time for them to do it and make sure you allow for the cost.

Right: Modern column radiators can suit an old house while offering the advantages of efficient heat output, reliability and ease of installation.

smaller-bore copper pipes have replaced the larger steel pipes of the past. When it comes to choosing radiators, for an old house there are two alternatives: either select a style that blends inconspicuously into the background or one that is a feature. The virtually flat radiators produced by some manufacturers merge perfectly into alcoves, fit under windows or echo panelling within a room. Equally, modern designer radiators can work well in old buildings because of their sheer creative form. Original or reproduction column radiators have a timeless quality that suits older houses, even those dating back many centuries. With all radiators, it is important to ensure that their size is capable of achieving the necessary heat output.

It is best not to disturb old cast iron radiators that are already installed, since moving them can cause damage. A pressure test is the most effective way of checking radiators for leaks. Before an old radiator is re-used, loose debris should be flushed out – this can often be achieved by forcing water through with a garden hose. Bear in mind that the connections between modern pipework and old radiators may be of different sizes; a good plumber should be able to obtain the relevant parts.

When it comes to boilers, a huge selection exists, so consult your heating engineer about the options. With old buildings, one of the most important considerations is the position of the flue, both within your home and externally. Its installation may cause damage to the fabric and can scar the exterior.

Electric storage heaters

Modern storage heaters are less ugly and more effective than those available in the past. Relatively easy to install,

Top tip: Turning up the heat

Always try to position radiators away from timber panelling and other joinery. Old buildings and furniture may be severely damaged by the drying effects of central heating systems; these can be reduced by leaving pots of water next to radiators to help maintain a natural level of humidity. When any heating system is newly installed, it should initially be used at a low output level to allow the building to acclimatise gently.

Above: Door panels are one of the items of joinery that may shrink and crack following installation of central heating. Turning up the heat slowly will help, but it may be worth waiting until the timber has settled before adding a final coat of paint.

either loose-laid or supplied as a mat; the latter is particularly good for small areas such as bathrooms. Both wet and dry systems are designed to suit most types of floor construction.

Before opting for UFH, it is important to consider the integrity of the building's fabric. Taking up a floor can have serious consequences. Not only may the character, history and structure of the building be destroyed but, if a concrete floor is laid or a damp proof membrane is introduced, the equilibrium of the structure may be upset, causing rising damp in the walls. For these reasons, such systems are most appropriate in situations where a floor is already being removed and re-laid for other reasons (➡ Why 'problems' occur, page 112).

they offer a reasonably economic way of heating an old house where electricity is the only source of energy. The downside is that because they use cheaper, off-peak power a separate electrical circuit has to be installed to supply them.

Underfloor heating

Underfloor heating (UFH) provides gentle, constant background heat and is better than the sudden bursts of intermittent heat provided by radiators. It can work particularly effectively within old buildings since it is discreet and excellent at heating large spaces with high ceilings. Ideal for cold floors such as stone or tile, it does away with the need for aesthetically inappropriate radiators and frees the wall space they would have occupied.

The predominant UFH system is wet, carrying warm water through continuous loops of special plastic pipe. Dry systems use electricity and consist of special cable,

Ducted systems

Ducted central heating, air conditioning and ventilation systems are really suitable only for larger houses. They can be installed in ceiling and floor voids with the flexible-supply tubing, which carries the warm or cool air, routed in and around the building's structure. Small outlet grilles are installed in the floors, ceilings or walls.

Although relatively expensive, these systems can be quiet and unobtrusive, and free up wall space. They create even room temperatures without draughts and warm up quickly; they are particularly good at heating larger rooms with high ceilings. The disadvantages are that the temperature cannot be varied in different rooms and grilles need to be positioned carefully in rooms with fireplaces to prevent drawing in smoke. Before going ahead with such a system, it is vital to ascertain that ducting and grilles can adequately be accommodated without damage to the building's fabric.

Above left: Wet underfloor heating systems utilise continuous loops of plastic pipe laid across the floor prior to screeding.

Above: If planning to install a wet underfloor heating system, think about the position of the manifold and do not underestimate the space it will take up.

14

Living for today and tomorrow

Today's lifestyles are very different from when the old houses we live in were built. We expect a lot more from our homes than our predecessors did. Balancing these needs with those of the building is not impossible, but it does require sensitivity.

Protecting your investment for tomorrow is all about the decisions you make today. Old buildings are a finite resource; as such, they become ever more desirable. Ill-thought through conversions or extensions can mar a house forever; when done well, they can enhance the building, adding both value and character.

Interestingly, many old buildings have attributes that make them perfect for twenty-first-century living. For example, houses designed by the Victorians can be extraordinarily successful in accommodating a modern family; they are sought after because they offer space, high ceilings, light, adaptable layouts and character. They also have potential, through careful conversion, to provide the extras that we see as important – such as en-suite shower rooms or space for a home office.

Most old buildings have a lot of life left in them. By adopting the right approach, using appropriate methods and maintaining them properly to ensure they do not deteriorate, we can enjoy them and leave them in good shape for future generations.

What is more, by keeping a building alive, all the embodied energy used within its construction is retained rather than wasted. It is worth remembering that caring for a house appropriately, using traditional materials,

Opposite: Good new design can work to striking effect in old buildings. Here, a new staircase has been combined with strong paint colours to complement and enhance the interior of an old house.

Above right: The repair of these terraced houses in Nelson, Lancashire, proves what can be done to give old buildings new life without destroying their integrity.

invariably means that you are having far less impact on the environment than if you were using modern, manufactured products or building new.

MAINTENANCE

It is surprisingly easy to ignore the fact that paint is peeling, a tile is slipping or a gutter is blocked. Sadly, problems are often noticed only when dampness has penetrated a building's fabric or when a leaking drain has caused subsidence.

Maintenance checklist

Left: If not promptly refixed or replaced, slipped and broken tiles put the fabric of a building in danger of water damage.

Try to look at all parts of the building from as many different vantage points as possible, such as from a neighbour's garden and by using binoculars. Where problems are evident, always deal with the underlying cause rather than rely on quick-fix solutions. Key areas are:

Roofs

> Examine regularly, and particularly after strong winds. Debris on the ground from broken slates and tiles often indicates a problem.
> Have dislodged slates and tiles reinstated promptly.
> Have the metal flashing and mortar fillets at junctions with chimneys and parapets inspected for signs of deterioration or movement.
> With thatched roofs, look for evidence of decay, particularly to the ridge.
> Where there is access to the roof's underside, look for leaks or damage to the roof covering.

Rainwater goods

> Look for blockages, cracks and leaks, especially during heavy rain.
> Clear gutters at least once a year – November is a good time, after leaves have fallen.

Drains

> Clear out gulleys beneath rainwater pipes and open the inspection covers of drains to check that the chamber beneath is not obstructed.
> If blockages regularly occur or a leak is suspected, seek expert advice.

Top: A broken downpipe is likely to result in a damp wall, and might be misinterpreted as 'rising damp' within the house.

Centre: Peeling paint, if left, will result in a large repair job, involving cutting out rotten timber and jointing in new.

Above: Plant growth can quickly take root in clogged gutters and cracks in damaged flaunching on chimney stacks.

Walls

> Ensure that ground levels around the building are not allowed to rise unduly.
> Clear airbricks using a stick.
> Repoint badly eroded mortar joints in walls and repair render.
> Re-apply limewash regularly.
> Monitor cracks.

Joinery

> Check windows, doors, fascias and barge boards regularly for cracked or rotten wood.
> Ensure that painted joinery is not flaking and allowing water to rot the timber.

Plant growth

> Ivy is invasive and will force open the joints of walls and damage roofs. It should be cut just above ground level and, once dead, removed.
> Keep trees near buildings under control, since they can cause subsidence, particularly on clay.

Chimneys and heating

> Ensure that chimneys are swept regularly.
> Check oil tanks and radiators for leaks, ensure that thermostats are working and have boilers serviced regularly.
> Where spark arresters have been fitted, ensure that they do not clog up.
> Check the stack within the roof space for open joints using a smoke pellet.

Pipes

> Both hot and cold water pipes should be adequately lagged.
> Check pipes from sinks and baths for leaks.
> Ensure that all stopcocks work.

Infestation and rot

> Annually check for signs of fungal and insect attack. Problems frequently occur under stairs and in cupboards, cellars and basements.

Fire

> Regularly clean and test smoke alarms and replace batteries.
> Check electrical wiring and, if necessary, get defects rectified by a qualified electrician. Vermin can gnaw through electrical installations, so clear away rubbish or food that may encourage nesting.

Just as with our own health, prevention is better than cure. Regular maintenance is the key to avoiding expensive and destructive problems later. This is not necessarily difficult, time-consuming or expensive, and relies largely on a commonsense approach.

BEING GREEN

Saving and generating energy is something we all need to consider, whatever age of house we live in. Old houses can be 'green': the principal consideration is to minimise the impact green measures will have on the function, structure, fabric and aesthetics of the building.

Careful thought needs to be given to the structural implications of mounting solar water-heating systems and photovoltaic panels on roofs or of attaching wind turbines. The associated cables and pipework need to be sensitively routed in order to cause the least amount of disruption to the building's fabric. Ground source heat pumps necessitate pipework being buried underground: think about the archaeological issues of digging within what may be an historic site.

Left: Ground-source heat pump systems require long, continuous loops of pipe to be laid underground to collect the heat. Where space is limited, bore holes may be an alternative.

Insulation

Creating a thermally insulated and airtight building envelope is the single most important means of cutting a home's energy use and therefore its carbon emissions.

Ventilation is equally important in all houses for a fresh, comfortable atmosphere and to prevent the build-up of condensation. It is even more important in old buildings which need to breathe; otherwise you may create a warm but damp interior. The trick is to provide as much insulation as possible while ensuring proper ventilation of the key areas, for instance sub-floor voids and uninhabited roof spaces.

Insulation materials

A variety of man-made insulation materials are available from DIY shops. Breathable natural materials also exist and are ideal for old buildings.

> **Cellulose fibre** Recycled newspaper that has been turned back into its raw fibrous state is particularly suited to loft insulation in old houses. Being 'loose-fill', the fibre completely fills all gaps around pipework, wiring and other obstructions, thus ensuring optimum insulation. Fire resistance is achieved through the addition of inorganic salts. Cellulose fibre is also resistant to biological and fungal attack, is treated against insects and is unattractive to vermin.

> **Wool** A natural fibre from a fully renewable resource, wool has the ability to absorb and release water vapour rapidly. When installed, the fibre adapts to the shape of rafters, joists and studs to provide a tight fit. Unlike glass fibre insulation, wool is not irritating to the skin, eyes or respiratory tract, so it can be installed without gloves or protective clothing. Insect proofing and fire resistance is achieved by the inclusion of naturally derived additives.

> **Hemp** Made from hemp and recycled cotton fibres, this is flexible and robust. Like wool, it can absorb and release water vapour. It poses no health hazard, makings installation and handling simple. Since the fibres are based on cellulose, there is no food source for insects or rodents. Treatment with a fire retardant meets building regulation requirements.

> **Reed** Natural reed, laid parallel and tightly bound using thin-gauge galvanised wire, is formed into a board and sold as a base for plastering internal walls and ceilings. It is an ideal means of adding a layer of insulation to the walls of timber-framed buildings.

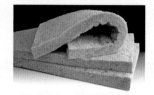

Top: Insulation made from recycled newspaper can be manually installed or mechanically blown into position to provide an even covering.

Second: Sheep's wool insulation is sold in 'batts' of various thicknesses.

Third: Like other natural insulation products, hemp can be laid without the need for protective clothing.

Fourth: Reed board is simply screwed into place. Use stainless steel screws and washers and plastic wall plugs to avoid thermal bridging.

Above: Extensions can sit comfortably with an old building, but to do so they must avoid poor pastiche and be in proportion to the original structure.

Right: New additions to historic buildings may be designed in a modern context. The 1970s house to the left here may be a well-considered piece of architecture, but it destroys the setting of the eighteenth-century gatehouse.

Right: At first glance this building appears to be classic eighteenth-century, yet the 'jettied' first floor gives away the much earlier timber-framed structure concealed behind. The Georgians added in a contemporary style; this building in Essex is much richer for it.

EXTENSIONS

Adaptation of a house over time is a natural part of its history. Even so, it is never wise to buy an old cottage and attempt to turn it into a mansion! If you need a lot more space, it is better to move house.

A good extension is all about appropriate scale and proportions both externally and internally, coupled with sensitive design and the use of suitable materials. It must enhance rather than compromise the existing building – for example, if your house is part of a terrace, consider the row as a whole rather than make alterations which spoil the appearance of the street.

Wherever possible, site an extension so that it does not detract from the proportions or key features of the existing building, and try to maintain the 'rhythm' of the architecture.

Rather than attempting to replicate an original architectural style, think about a contemporary look. The Georgians never tried to replicate the Tudor style when adding to an older house; as a result, we have inherited 'layered' buildings which are fascinating to explore and beautiful to the eye.

Good new design that is honest to its own period can work well alongside an old building and ensures that the two ages are clearly distinguishable. This approach can also make for exciting internal living spaces which suit today's lifestyle and add something of value that future generations will enjoy. As with any work to an old building, try to ensure reversibility so that the extension could be removed with minimum damage to the historic fabric. This is a particular consideration when creating a means of entry into the new part of the building; rather than knocking holes in original walls, try to use existing door or window openings to minimise damage.

Modern building regulations mean that it is unlikely you will be able to build an extension using exactly the same methods as those employed in the construction of the original house. It is worth considering modern ecological alternatives. Hemp, straw bales and clay blocks are all options that can be combined with lime mortars and renders.

Due to differential settlement, problems can occur when a new extension, with the deep foundations required by building regulations, is built next to an old house with shallow foundations. It is a good idea to design the junction to allow for some movement to take place.

of your staircase until the end, since you may find that you simply cannot fit it in. You might even find that it takes up so much space on the lower floor that it cancels out the space gained by the loft conversion.

Constructing a room in a loft space often involves work to the roof and floor structure. It can result in the loss of historic timber and the introduction of steelwork or extra timber to carry the loads imposed. Generally, a structural engineer should be consulted to provide calculations and drawings. Joists, rafters and other roof timbers are there for a purpose: never cut through them unless adequate alternative support has been provided. A key consideration is to design any additional structural elements so that they can be introduced without disturbing the existing ceilings and decorations below. Particular care should be taken over fragile and historic plasterwork; hammering should be kept to a minimum.

Often the challenge is to provide sufficient insulation to a previously uninsulated roof. Ideally, there must be a

Above: The extension to this large Victorian semi-detached house features a clerestory, using traditional materials including stone and lead in conjunction with load-bearing steel and modern glazing. The roof extends to form a shaded terrace, with all roof drainage via the hanging chain.

Right: This alternating tread stair is an approved way of providing a staircase where there is insufficient room for a standard arrangement.

Conservatories are often seen as an easy way of providing extra space, but they are not always a good solution, historically or aesthetically. Their use dates from Victorian times when they were attached to large houses; they were too expensive to be found on more humble dwellings.

LOFT CONVERSIONS

Converting a loft may, at first sight, seem to have much less impact on the appearance of an old house than an extension. The disadvantage is that it can put tremendous pressures on the building's existing fabric, structure and layout. Even with a big house, think carefully before embarking on such a project: loft conversion specialists may be good at loft conversions, but are not necessarily good with old buildings. Before starting a conversion, think what it is going to be used for. If it is just for storage, a conventional drop-down loft-ladder may be adequate. Always avoid putting heavy loads on ceilings that have not been reinforced.

Even where loft space can easily be converted, the big challenge is likely to be finding a place to put the staircase. Consider the structural and aesthetic implications of its installation – you may have to sacrifice a bedroom or a landing to fit it in. Any new staircase will have to meet building regulations, including pitch, headroom and handrail heights. Never leave the design

Top: Only the purlins and ridge board have been left exposed in this loft conversion, enabling the spaces between the rafters to be insulated. A previously blocked window has not been reinstated.

Above: Positioning rooflights on the inner slopes of the roof conceals them from view externally, yet provides light and a view of the sky from within the house.

Right: Damp is not the only problem in cellars and basements. To make them usable it is often necessary to tidy up the services that enter the house at this point.

free flow of air around roof timbers. There is a great temptation to leave rafters exposed, but this involves either insulating above the rafters and raising the height of the roof, or insulating between the rafters and preventing adequate ventilation. By far the least invasive solution is to apply insulation to the underside of rafters, or batten out the rafters to provide sufficient depth for insulation to be fitted between them, in conjunction with the insertion of a modern ceiling.

Adding an additional floor generally means that a clear, fireproof, escape route is required. The door at the top or bottom of the new staircase will need to be fire-resistant and other doors on to the landings and hall will have to be upgraded to fire doors. Be sure to think this through if you have a beautifully proportioned landing and historic doors.

In the loft, a suitable window has to be provided as a means of escape. Think carefully about the position of windows within a roof space in relation to the external appearance of the building and to the doors and windows below.

CELLARS AND BASEMENTS

The difference between a cellar and a basement is often somewhat blurred. The former is generally an under-ground room for storage. The latter is usually an area once used by servants, and is frequently, but not always, partially above ground level.

Before turning a cellar or basement into a living space, consider how practical it will be and accept its limitations. If the room is to be habitable, requirements such as damp-proofing, ventilation, access, headroom, lighting and fire protection all have to be considered. Bear in mind the structural considerations, the risk of flooding and the costs involved. The various methods used to make the space habitable may destroy the wonderful character of an intact basement, so think carefully about whether your old building can really take this level of intrusion.

With good cross-ventilation and little interference, an original cellar can make a great wine store or freezer room, and often provides the ideal space in which to fit bulky boilers and tanks.

Damp

Damp is likely to be a potential problem, since many basements and cellars were never designed to be habit-able spaces. Even where a damp-proofing system has already been correctly installed, problems may arise in the future. Where walls have been tanked at basement level, dampness may be driven up the masonry to the ground floor and cause rising damp. Condensation can be particularly problematic, since walls underground tend to be cold to the touch. Ventilation is vital and must be achieved either through natural means or by the installation of mechanical systems. Where the problem is severe, a dehumidifier can help. Avoid using products that stop moisture escaping, such as vinyl wallpaper, impermeable paints, foam-backed carpets and linoleum.

Damp-proofing systems

Three main methods are employed to make cellars and basements habitable. All require a thorough understanding of the problem and careful execution of the work to be successful.

Ventilated dry lining is usually employed in situations where damp is not excessive. Using a special dimpled plastic sheet, a ventilated air gap is created between the walls and an inner dry lining, while a screed is laid over a damp-proof membrane on the floor. The system has the advantages of taking up minimal space and allowing the walls to breathe, while causing little damage to the fabric of the building; it is also reversible. Good ventilation is vital. Care must be taken not to puncture the materials accidentally when shelves or electrical services are fitted.

Above: Dry lining membranes must be carefully fixed to ensure that dampness cannot penetrate. The surface is dimpled to allow for ventilation and the drainage of moisture between the membrane and the wall.

Drained cavity systems involve creating a room within a room. This is achieved by constructing floors and blockwork walls which are totally isolated from the building's main structure by damp-proof membranes. The cavity formed allows water to be collected and drained or pumped away. The disadvantages are that the blockwork takes up valuable space and, for its long-term efficiency, the drainage or pumping system must be maintained.

Tanking employs a waterproof material to seal the walls and floor totally, quite literally forming a tank. The work is carried out either inside or outside the building. When undertaken inside, there is a danger that the hydrostatic pressure from water in the surrounding subsoil may force off the tanking layer. To prevent this, an inner block wall is sometimes constructed to hold the material in place. Of all the systems, this is probably the most invasive and the most likely to cause problems in the longer term.

Right: Bathrooms can easily date, especially when installed in an old house, but here a timeless quality has been achieved.

Always react to any dampness in a cellar or basement quickly to prevent the problem getting worse. Leaking water mains and sewers in the street can be a cause. Problems may occur if a neighbour has had a basement or cellar tanked or a damp-proof course has been injected into walls.

BATHROOMS

Installing new bathrooms in old buildings needs careful thought. Look at where the existing soil pipes and drains run and, wherever possible, try to site new bathrooms to link in with them. While pumps and macerators may make it possible to put your bathroom virtually any-where, the pipework that accompanies such equipment can be bulky and ugly.

Original bathroom fittings are a valuable part of the history of a house, so try to keep them. Old cast iron baths can be overhauled and re-enamelled. As floors are rarely level in old buildings, consider wall-mounted lavatories and basins, and baths with adjustable feet.

Below: A rare find, an original basin, mirror and tiling unit of this quality is well worth retaining.

Below right: Simple but elegant, this scullery offers modern convenience with a period feel.

KITCHENS AND UTILITY ROOMS

Incorporating the requirements of a modern kitchen sympathetically within an old house is something of a challenge, but not impossible. The first priority is to avoid disturbing the fabric of the building more than necessary.

Both traditional and modern looks can work well in an old house, but it is often preferable to opt for free-standing items rather than a fitted kitchen. When walls, floors and ceiling are uneven, installing standard units and worktops may prove a nightmare. Try to design your kitchen so that when it needs renewing, as it will do, stripping it out will not damage the building. A free-standing dresser will not only provide storage space and look good but may cost no more than fitted units. In reality, it is almost impossible to escape some elements being fitted, since the sink and appliances require connection to water, gas or electrical supplies; a free-standing range for cooking minimises this problem.

Below: This kitchen mixes traditional forms with contemporary design. The boxed-in soil pipe at high level is decorated with a play on words.

The provision of water, electricity and gas within a kitchen is easier, and generally also cheaper and tidier, if the units requiring them are grouped together. Existing drainage arrangements should be noted: less disruption will be involved if the drains from the kitchen are on the same side of the building as those from bathrooms.

The extraction of smells and steam is important, so a cooker hood with an extractor fan should be installed wherever possible; take care, however, to minimise damage when cutting holes for vents in walls or ceilings. Where it is difficult to vent a hood externally, consider a version that filters and recirculates the air within the room. This will not be as efficient, so a separate extractor fan should also be fitted.

A heat alarm, rather than a smoke alarm, should be installed in a kitchen, with a fire extinguisher and fire blanket ready to hand.

When an old-style sink and wooden draining board exist but are not suitable for the kitchen, consider installing them instead in a utility room. This is just one example of how original features may usefully be retained.

Acknowledgements

Our first and most considerable debt is to Gillian Darley, Liz Drury and Philip Venning, without whom we would never have embarked upon or completed this project, and John Nicoll who enthusiastically took up the idea.

Special mention must go to Anthony Goode, for teaching and passing on so many practical skills and never being afraid to experiment, and to Rory Young, for the inspiration of his completed works.

To see the book through to fruition we have had valuable help from a great many individuals. They have drawn from their considerable collective knowledge to give us patient encouragement and advice with unfailing generosity. Jim Boutwood, Douglas Kent, Matthew Slocombe and Michael Tutton have read and re-read our manuscript while Matt Green, Jeff Orton, Patrick Stow and Roger Scanlan have advised on the chapters relating to their particular areas of expertise. Libby Fellingham, with great forbearance, created the splendid illustrations while Jane Havell, in her editing and design, has painstakingly brought all our efforts together.

Many, many others have given more general help and technical advice. These include: Rachel Bower, Hannah Diment, Sarah Evans, Tony Evans, Jean Goode, Kate Griffin, Peter McCurdy, Andy Millmore, Ian Pritchett, Robin Stummer, Caroline Turner and Sean Wheatley. Thanks go to them all and to those we have omitted we must apologise.

We would also like to acknowledge the help of all the builders, craftspeople and experts we have worked with on our own projects, some of whom have patiently posed for photographs.

Finally, we must thank our families who have borne the brunt of our deadlines and preoccupations – above all, Mandy and Christina Suhr and Betty and Peter Hunt and, in particular, our partners, Elizabeth and Richard, who have been ceaseless in their encouragement and tolerance.

Picture credits

References are to page numbers

Aldershaw Handmade Tiles 62 bottom left, 62 bottom right

Peter Ayley 197

Cliff Blundell 111 top

Ian Bristow 166 bottom

Richard Cain 86 right, 87 bottom right

Charnwood 123 bottom right

Dimplex UK 191 left

Excel Fibre Technology 191 top right

Alan Forbes/Richard Murphy Architects 193 top

Fleur Gordon 61 all

Roger Hunt 10 bottom, 12 left, 13 bottom, 17 left, 22, 23 bottom, 35, 39, 52 top left, 57, 62 top, 67 top right, 67 bottom left, 69 top right, 94, 98 right, 104 top, 106 bottom, 109, 115 all, 120, 123 bottom left, 134 all, 136 centre left, 137 top, 140 left, 144 bottom left, 145, 151 top left, 157 bottom right, 170 bottom, 176, 179 left, 181 left centre, 181 bottom right, 181 bottom centre, 182 centre, 182 bottom right, 183 bottom right, 184 centre, 185 top, 185 centre, 186 centre, 187 left, 190 top

Douglas James/Uponor Housing Solutions 187 centre, 187 right

Nick Joyce 103, 103 survey drawings

Plant Fibre Technology 191 third from top right

Sandtoft 83 bottom left, 83 bottom right

Second Nature UK 81 bottom, 191 second from top right

Matthew Slocombe 122 left, 177

SPAB 4, 17 right

Patrick Stow 67 bottom right

Marianne Suhr 10 top, 11 top, 12 right, 15 all, 16 top, 16 bottom right, 18, 19, 21, 24, 25 all, 26, 27, 28 all, 29 top, 29 bottom, 30 all, 31 all, 33, 36, 37 all, 40 all, 41 all, 42, 44 all, 45, 46, 47 all, 48 all, 50 all, 52 centre, 52 bottom centre, 53 all, 54 all, 55 all left, 56 left, 58 all, 59 all, 60 all, 64, 65, 66 bottom, 68 all, 70 all, 71 all, 72, 73 all, 74 bottom, 75, 76, 77, 79 all, 81 top left, 81 top right, 83 top, 84, 85 all, 86 left, 87 top left, 87 top right, 88 all, 89, 90 all, 91 right, 92, 93, 95, 96, 97 all, 98 top left, 98 bottom, 99 all, 100, 102, 104 bottom row, 104 centre right, 105 top left, 105 bottom left, 106 top, 108, 112 bottom, 114 bottom, 117 top, 117 right, 119 all, 121, 122 right, 123 top, 123 top centre, 124 all, 125 all, 126 all, 127, 128, 129 all, 130, 131, 133 top left, 133 bottom left, 135 all, 136 top, 136 bottom left, 136 bottom right, 137 bottom, 139 top left, 139 centre left, 139 bottom left, 140 bottom centre, 140 bottom right, 141, 142 all, 143 bottom right, 144 top left, 144 bottom right, 147 bottom, 151 bottom left, 151 bottom centre, 151 bottom right, 152 all, 153, 154 all, 155 all, 156 top, 157 top right, 159 all, 160 all, 161, 162, 163, 164 top left, 164 bottom left, 165 all, 166 top, 167 all, 168 all, 169 all, 170 top, 172 all, 173 all, 174 all, 175 all, 178 bottom left, 178 bottom right, 178 centre, 179 bottom left, 179 bottom right, 179 top right, 179 centre right, 181 top right, 182 top, 183 top left, 183 top right, 183 bottom left, 184 bottom left, 184 top right, 184 bottom right, 185 bottom, 186 top left, 186 top right, 186 bottom right, 189 all, 190 top left, 190 centre, 190 bottom, 191 bottom right, 192 all, 193 bottom, 194 top, 196 left

Andrew Townsend 188

Philip Venning 9 all, 11 bottom, 13 top, 14 all, 16 bottom left, 20, 23 top, 29 centre, 32, 38 all, 49, 51 all, 52 middle left, 52 bottom left, 52 bottom right, 55 bottom right, 56 right, 63 all, 66 top, 69 top left, 69 bottom left, 74 top, 78 all, 80, 82 all, 83 middle, 91 left, 111 bottom, 112 top, 113, 116, 117 bottom left, 132, 133 right, 139 bottom right, 143 top, 143 bottom left, 150 bottom right, 156 bottom left, 156 bottom right, 158, 171, 178 top, 181 top left, 181 top centre, 181 bottom left, 182 left, 182 bottom left

Wykamol Group 194 bottom right, 195 left

Rory Young 8, 34, 43, 105 right, 110, 114 top, 146, 147 top, 148, 149, 150 top, 150 bottom left, 157 left, 164 right, 194 bottom left, 195 right, 196 right

Illustrations in chapters 3, 4 and 8 by Marianne Suhr. All remaining illustrations drawn by Libby Fellingham with assistance from Marianne Suhr. Colouring of all illustrations by Libby Fellingham.

Index